Valley of Diamonds

Marie-Louise von Franz, Honorary Patron

**Studies in Jungian Psychology
by Jungian Analysts**

Daryl Sharp, General Editor

VALLEY OF DIAMONDS
Adventures in *Number and Time*
with Marie-Louise von Franz

J. GARY SPARKS

For my grandfathers.
There is a dream dreaming us.—the Kalahari Bushmen.
—Laurens van der Post, *Jung and the Story of Our Time,* p. 13.

Library and Archives Canada Cataloguing in Publication

Sparks, J. Gary (John Gary), 1948-
Valley of diamonds: adventures in number and time
With Marie-Louise von Franz / J. Gary Sparks

(Studies in Jungian psychology by Jungian analysts; 127)

Includes bibliographical references and index.
ISBN 978-1-894574-28-0

1. Franz, Marie-Louise von, 1915-1998. Zahl und Zeit..

2. Symbolism (Psychology). I. Title. II Series: Studies in
    Jungian psychology by Jungian analysts; 127.

BF173.5.S63 2010   150.19'54   C2009-905631-3

INNER CITY BOOKS
Box 1271, Station Q, Toronto, ON M4T 2P4, Canada
Telephone (416) 927-0355 / Fax (416) 924-1814
Web site: www.innercitybooks.net
E-mail: admin@innercitybooks.net

Honorary Patron: Marie-Louise von Franz.
Publisher and General Editor: Daryl Sharp.
Senior Editor: Victoria Cowan.
Office Manager: Scott Milligen, D.PC.

INNER CITY BOOKS was founded in 1980 to promote the
understanding and practical application of the work of C.G. Jung.

Cover: Spirale imperfetto, oil on canvas, 96 x 126 cm., 2006, by Claudia
N. Nolte, California & Europe.

Printed and bound in Canada by Thistle Printing Limited

Contents

PART III: The Field of the Collective Unconscious and Its Inner Dynamism

See final pages for descriptions of other Inner City Titles

Illustrations and Credits

Introduction

A Pocket Full of Diamonds

Carl Jung told the dream to Olga Fröbe-Kapteyn. In 1933 she had founded the Eranos conferences which met at Casa Gabriella, her villa on the beautiful Lake Maggiore near Ascona, in southern Switzerland. At these events scholars from all walks of life—the sciences, religion, philosophy, Jungian psychology—met together with other attendees and presented papers on matters of human interest and world culture. Jung was always a central participant, though otherwise the subject matter of the conferences was not specifically Jungian.[1] Late in his life, he recounted to the Eranos hostess a dream he had had several years earlier during a serious illness:

> It seemed as though I were in a valley full of diamonds, and I was allowed to fill my pockets with diamonds and to take as many in my hands as I could carry—but no more than that. I have a few years left to live, and I'd like to tell as much as I can of what I understood then, when I was ill, but I realize I won't succeed in expressing more than an infinitesimal part, that I'll not be able to show more than one or two diamonds, although my pockets are full of them.[2]

Jung began his major writing in 1944 at the age of sixty-nine. These works include: "The Psychology of the Transference" (1946), *Aion* (1951), "Answer to Job" (1952), "Synchronicity: An Acausal Connecting Principle" (1952), and *Mysterium Coniunctions* (1955-56), not to mention a hefty corpus of personal and professional correspondence.[3]

Those books, essays, and letters offered, in a rich and precise form, his

---

[1] Eranos Homepage; www.eranosfoundation.org.

[2] Mircea Eliade, *Journal I: 1945-1955*, p. 193.

[3] "The Psychology of the Transference" is in vol. 16 of Jung's *Collected Works* (hereafter CW); *Aion* is CW 9i; "Answer to Job" is in CW 11; "Synchronicity: An Acausal Connecting Principle" is in CW 8; and *Mysterium Coniunctionis* is CW 14. Jung's correspondence has been published in his *Letters*: vols.1 and 2. Edward Edinger's *The New God-Image* is an excellent introduction to selected themes in Jung's second volume of letters.

essential understanding of psychological healing. To a significant extent, this was based on a metaphorical interpretation of the imagery expressed throughout the writings of medieval alchemists. Jung had become aware of how the process of emotional maturation went beyond the traditional framework of a psychological worldview. Questions of religious experience and the awful condition of organized religion; themes reflecting the historical development of our community, indeed sometimes of our nation and world; issues regarding our role in such events; problems in our grasp of nature, of biology, of disease; stumbling blocks in science and technology as well as distortions in our relations to them; challenges in appreciating all facets of the arts, also of world myth, which emerge when they are seen though the lens of dream logic; the sufferings and inspirations of uniquely creative persons seeking to find and bring their work to the world—all of these had come to occupy Jung's attention.[4]

In particular he showed that when we focus on our inner processes, when we are honestly devoted to, unraveling the inner world of our dreams and fantasies, they will point past our merely personal life. Their meaning brings us into a new and important relation to the outer world. We learn that the inside and outside are not really separate entities. He painted that in a broad stroke:

> We are driven to the conclusion that the space-time continuum, including mass, is psychically relative—in other words, that it forms a unity with the unconscious psyche.[5] Accordingly, there must be phenomena which can be explained only in terms of a psychic relativity of space, time, and mass.[6]

The dream world and the outer world of objective matter, of real events in time and space, share a continuum. Our grasp of them as separate entities is incomplete. Somehow they "smear" into each other; their

---

[4] See especially C.G. Jung, "Address on the Occasion of the Founding of the C.G. Jung Institute, Zürich, 24 April 1948," in *The Symbolic Life*, CW 18, pars. 1129ff.

[5] In Jung's words: "By psyche I understand the totality of all psychic processes, conscious as well as unconscious." (C.G. Jung, *Psychological Types*, CW 6, par. 797. For a descriptive account see Jolande Jacobi, *The Psychology of C.G. Jung*, pp. 5ff.)

[6] "Address on the Occasion of the Founding," *The Symbolic Life*, CW 18, par. 1133.

perceived separateness is only relatively true. This is suggested by the appearance in dreams of themes external to our everyday living, often themes about parts of life with which it seems we have no personal connection. How is it that we can dream about the state of theology and religion,[7] when we are not particularly tied to these concerns—or of problems in history,[8] the sufferings of our community,[9] issues in science and technology,[10] for example? How can an unknown neurological ailment be anonymously diagnosed from a dream?[11] How can dream images appear in the body?[12] And how can an inner dream image show up in concrete form in an event in the physical world—in a way that defies all probability? That is to ask, how is a synchronicity,[13] a word we will see much more of in the pages ahead, even possible? What is the link between inside and outside, between our "inner" psychology and "outer" matter?

This is a puzzle that Jung worked on to the end of his life, realizing, finally, that he had to leave the question open. Marie-Louise von Franz, widely regarded as Jung's most original and accurate interpreter, describes Jung saying to her:

> Now I have the feeling that I've hit my head against the ceiling. I can't get any farther than this.[14]

He thought possibly the link between the two worlds was to be found in a parallelism between the presence of numbers in the unconscious, that is,

---

[7] C.G. Jung, *Dream Analysis: Notes of the Seminar*, pp. 317ff.

[8] See Jung, *Visions: Notes of the Seminar*, esp. pp. 823-874, 1022f., 1269; also Jung, *Nietzsche's* Zarathustra*: Notes of the Seminar*, and James Kirsch, *The Reluctant Prophet*.

[9] M.-L. von Franz, *Psyche and Matter*, pp. 165ff.

[10] Wolfgang Pauli and C.G. Jung, *Atom and Archetype*.

[11] R. Lockhart, "Cancer and Myth and Dreams," *Spring 1977*, pp. 8ff.

[12] See Anne Maguire, *Seven Deadly Sins* and *Skin Disease: A Message from the Soul*; also Alfred Ziegler, *Archetypal Medicine*.

[13] I'll define the term in chapter 1. For the moment consider synchronicity a meaningful coincidence between an inner state of mind and an outer event. A classic example in the Jungian literature is the "scarab" event: C.G. Jung, "Synchronicity: An Acausal Connecting Principle," in *The Structure and Dynamics of the Psyche*, CW 8, par. 843.

[14] *Psyche and Matter*, p. 37. She describes this conversation in less detail in the Preface to *Number and Time*.

in dreams, and the presence of numerical relations in the structure, composition, and functioning of matter—as reflected in the theories of physics. Von Franz continues her account of their conversation:

> Jung's idea was that one should study the individuality of these numbers—be interested in what each has that the others have not, rather than what they have in common. He made a note three inches square, on which he wrote: one, the all; two, the only even prime number; three, the first uneven prime number, the sum of one and two, the first triangular number; four, the first quadrangular number, the first square number, and so on. Then he said he couldn't do it; he felt too old. That was about two years before his death. He gave me that little paper—he said, "I give it to you."[15]

This was the inception of von Franz's *Number and Time*.[16] On that account she describes her efforts in the book to probe the symbolism of the first four integers:

> I counted to four and tried to assemble the qualities of each in psychology, mythology, physics, and mathematics; and it is, to me at least, quite clear that they *really have the same function*—that if you compare the role of three in mathematics and physics, there is a similar function in psychological and symbolic manifestation. Then I discovered, to my amazement, that Chinese mathematics were completely built on this idea of the quality of numbers.[17]

Summary of *Number and Time*

Chapters 1, 2, and 3 present the first main thesis of her book. In chapter 1, von Franz reminds us that both depth psychology and quantum physics were born at the beginning of the twentieth century. Not only will she be investigating parallels in their discoveries, but also how their subject matter, the inner psychological and outer physical, may seem separate but share a commonality.[18] Thanks to Jung's concept of synchronicity,

---

[15] Ibid., p. 163.

[16] Ibid., p. 164.

[17] Ibid.

[18] Hence the subtitle of her book: "Reflections Leading Toward a Unification of Depth

we recognize that at certain moments the inner psychological and the outer material reflect the same symbolic image—alluding to some sort of unity to life. This unity is normally experienced in two ways, inner and outer, that is, in dreams and in reality, but it is also sometimes experienced as a synchronous singularity. Obviously she will discuss what synchronicity is throughout the book—if this is a word unfamiliar to us at the moment.

Chapter 2 explores the symbolic and qualitative character of number. Of consequence is how the material and mental parts of life can be connected. The theory she'll be proposing is that number, qualitatively understood, unites the two realms. She introduces that idea provisionally in this chapter by noting that we all have a life story which we are born with—for Jung identity is inborn as a potentiality—and that story evolves successively over the course of life: there is a first part, a second part, a third part, etc. Number symbolism is thus intimately tied to the unfolding of our life's story and meaning.

Chapter 3 appraises more of this "numerical" aspect of life—the role of numbers and number symbolism that emerges in dreams, for example. Then she investigates the role of numbers in the theories about the intricacies of the material world and the atom. The parallel role of number in our life's story and in the material world, she posits, is the reason that dreams and outer events can meet and express a similar idea in synchronistic moments. This point is the most important idea developed in part I, chapters 1 through 3.

In the next section of the book, part II, von Franz examines the symbolism of numbers in psychology, myth, physics, and mathematics. One of her points is to show how numbers are symbols with an exceedingly important role in dreaming. They are representative of characteristic stages of the inborn healing process that Jung discovered early in his career, finalizing that idea by the time he was about fifty-three. Jung's discovery is a salient theme in all of part II, chapters 4 through 7. She also demonstrates in what way the psychological role of numbers as symbols is often similar to the role of those numbers in physics and subatomic

Psychology and Physics."

processes. The most important point in part II is her explication of the character of numbers as symbols of the Self's transformation through various, though somewhat predictable, stages. All of these complicated-sounding terms are explained along the way.

Parts I and II thus present the two main theses of the book: 1) the analogous role of numbers in psychology and the processes of matter; and 2) the role of numbers as symbols of the unfolding of selfhood in psychological healing, growth, and maturation.

Part III, chapters 8 and 9, are an interlude. Chapter 8 discusses numbers as fields, that is, symbols; chapter 9 discusses numbers' relation to Jung's concept of psychic energy, another description of the Self's transformation already outlined in terms of number symbolism in part II.

Part IV turns to the connection between matter and our inner psychological processes, not from the point of view of numbers, as previously, but from the point of view of images, looking at images of the connection between outer matter and the inner dream-world. The main image she surveys is the dual mandala (the mandala is a "magic" circular image known in the history of religion as an aid to meditation); here the unity of the world is described by two images which together make up the whole. Chapters 10 and 11 portray the two sides of the dual mandala image. Chapter 12 examines how "chance" lies behind those moments when the inner world and the outer world act in tandem, namely during a synchronistic moment. Previously the book looked at numbers as the link between the two poles of life; now it considers the nature of meaningful chance which makes it possible for numbers to provide that link.

Chapter 13 discusses the creative potential of time expressed, for example, in antiquity in the Greek word *kairos*. Chapter 14 is another interlude. Chapter 15 examines the union or *coniunctio* (the alchemists' Latin word for union) aspect of these unitary, that is, synchronistic, moments. Chapters 13-15 make up part V, the last section of the book.

We will pay particular attention to parts I and II, because they suggest the main tenets of *Number and Time*, with the other parts and chapters in the book circling around the two main ideas. Having grasped the two "big points" of the book, we will find the remainder of von Franz's discussion falls into place as an enumeration of two basic ideas. The book's inner coherence will make its assimilation gratifying.

Inasmuch as this book is intended as an introduction to *Number and Time,* its format parallels the parts and chapters of von Franz's book.

A Jewel of Jung's Legacy

Jung began his work as a psychologist sifting through his own dreams and those of his patients—finding how it is that we can heal emotionally from the inside out when life has become confusing and unmanageable. Jung's was an inner inquiry at first, though it wasn't long before he was forced to entertain considerations that he knew would find no resonance among traditional scientists, nor among traditional religious believers. At issue is the breaking down of walls that have separated the Western view of reality into false either-ors, and hence also at issue is the building up of a more comprehensive understanding of life.

Continuing this rebuilding in her book *Number and Time*, von Franz has undertaken to carry on Jung's work of fashioning the future viewpoint. It is my hope to make her work more accessible: not to create a substitute for her ever-thoughtful and searching prose, but to build a bridge crossing into her very generous inquiry.

Surely this inquiry into the unity of outer matter and inner psychological processes is one of the diamonds Jung found in the valley that night, another proudly-faceted jewel of his legacy to humankind.

Marie-Louise-von Franz and C.G. Jung (about 1960).

PART I
Number as the Common Ordering Factor
of Psyche and Matter

Chapter 1

The Problem of the Unity of Psyche and Matter

I will summarize each chapter before considering it in detail. Recognizing the chapter's basic idea will orient us to the particulars of von Franz's discussion that follow.

The first chapter explores how the images that appear in a synchronicity, those coincidences that fall into our daily lives, are part of the larger pattern of our existence. Von Franz additionally suggests that this pattern can be understood in a numerical way.

Two New Disciplines

She begins *Number and Time* by providing the historical context for her book. She observes that two new disciplines emerged at the beginning of the twentieth century, depth psychology and quantum physics. That is no accident:[19] both represent an extension of human knowledge, and they have significant features in common. Although one deals with the inner world of the psyche and one with the outer world of matter, their insights possess an amazing correspondence. Let's look at each briefly.

Jung's discovery at the beginning of the last century had to do with an inborn process of psychological healing—an intrinsic capacity for emotional healing within each of us. He recognized that its characteristics were not determined by an individual's past experiences; the process had an independent life of its own. That such a dynamic existed flew in the face of the psychoanalytic world then, and now, since Freud's view was

---

[19] Jungian psychology was developed in Zürich during the years 1913 until 1928; quantum mechanics was developed in Copenhagen during the years 1913 until 1927. See my book, *At the Heart of Matter: Synchronicity and Jung's Spiritual Testament*, pp. 29ff.

that everything "psychological" that is inside us was a result of early experiences. Jung observed that this healing process, once activated, required only that we cooperate with it—not that we understand its "cause." The nature of Jung's perspective concerning our in-born capacity for psychological healing will occupy us throughout this book.

A cardinal feature of quantum physics, the other momentous discovery that von Franz refers to, parallels Jung's discovery. When, for example, a chemical element in gas form receives heat or electricity, the atoms in the gas are naturally energized. The quantum physicists realized that the electrons in the atoms are zapped out of their original orbit around the nucleus of the atom and move to an orbit of a higher energy level. The activated electron may jump up one orbital level or more orbital levels. The route the energized electron takes may be a direct one to its final orbit or it may pass along the way through an intermediate orbit. Its path can never be predicted. (Figure 1a)

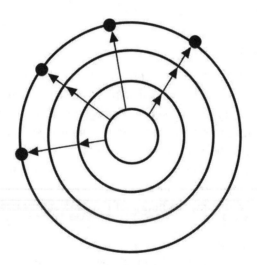

a) an energized electron moves
to a higher orbit in unpredictable jumps

Figure 1a.

The energized electron at the higher orbital level will be unstable since it is out of its "home" orbit. So it falls back to its original orbit, giving off energy in a particular wavelength of light. That is why electrically energized gasses glow—think of a neon sign. But again there is the puzzling part. Once it loses its energy at the higher orbit, it will fall back to its original orbit in a completely unpredictable fashion. It may return directly or pass through the lower orbits, until it reaches its original state.

The way the electron moves back down energy levels is again utterly unpredictable. (Figure 1b) The trajectory of an excited electron cannot be foreseen from the energy that initiated its movement.

That contradicts everything in classical physics which says, for example, that if we release a bowling ball and we hit another bowling ball, the first bowling ball will cause the movement of the second bowling ball, and that we can calculate the resulting movement. There is a cause and an effect. In quantum physics, however, that causal logic breaks down. The path of an energized electron is independent of what set the electron in motion.

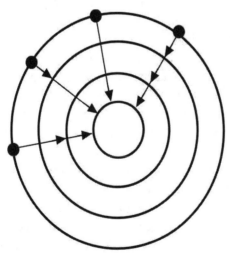

b) an electron losing energy moves back
to its original orbit in unpredictable jumps

Figure 1b.

Both psychology and physics hit upon the limits of causal thinking in their respective disciplines. This is important for us as psychologists because Jung's approach doesn't try to cause growth; it tries to respond to it—as we will pursue more closely in part II. In any case, the limits of causality as an explanatory principle is one of the discoveries in the early nineteen hundreds that both disciplines share and why von Franz starts her book with a reference to it. There is also another significant and separately discovered parallel insight into the workings of psychic and physical nature shared by the two disciplines. A description of that will be considered shortly.

Refining Archetypes

As with Freud, Jung begins his inquiry into human nature with a consideration of instincts. But the parallels between psychology and physics led him to reevaluate his grasp of how we are motivated. These parallels brought to mind the role of matter in conscious living. The link between the domain of psychology, inner psychic processes, and the domain of physics, matter, struck Jung forcibly. Through this he was led to reevaluate the foundation of his psychological theory.

What are instincts? Instincts are inborn, inherited patterns of behavior. They are conservative. Read love poetry now, read love poetry from a thousand years ago, it is very similar. Read love poetry two thousand years ago, it is very much the same. Aggression, another major instinct, acts similarly across cultural lines and periods of history. The basic patterns of instincts don't change.

But, when we are in the midst of an instinctive pattern of behavior, we are also *experiencing* that pattern of behavior. So an instinct brings with it the possibility of understanding the behavior that we are engaged in, both from the conscious point of view (our awareness of thoughts and emotions) and from the unconscious point of view (the appearance in our dreams of images symbolizing the instinct). For Jung there is a biological pole to instinct, and there is a *mental* pole to instinct: there is the instinctual act and there is the conscious and unconscious registering of the instinctual act.

Now comes Jung's early contribution to psychological theory through his considering the way dreams symbolize instinct in the form of images. Instincts are often symbolized by animals. The sex instinct may be represented in a dream as a lascivious cat, for example. Or the instinct of aggression may appear as an angry dog. Jung recognized that the images which portray instinct are, however, *not* always static; they can and will change over time *if and when we try to understand them in dreamwork.* Dreams generate images of the instincts that are moving us at any given time, and when we work with those images consciously and patiently, they begin to show an "intelligence" and seem to know of their own possibility of transformation. In other words, consciousness can initiate a process of change within the instinct through understanding the images which symbolize it. The lascivious cat may change into a beautiful woman—lust thereby developing into human tenderness; the angry dog, once properly attended to, may metamorphose into a valuable protector and companion—rage thereby developing into a sense of clear boundaries. The process is slow and laborious, but dreamwork shows how, when the images that symbolize instincts are taken seriously, the instincts thus represented are capable of change *in a direction they apparently know on their own.* The traditional view of instincts ignores their capacity to change and their apparent inner intelligence.

Jung wrote about these two poles—instinct and image—using the simile of a light spectrum, where the instincts correspond to the red light end of the spectrum and the image would correspond to violet.[20] This is Jung's first description of psychic energy: psychological energy is made up of an instinctual pole and an image pole, an act and the possibility of experiencing and symbolizing that act. In terms of his simile, psychological energy is likened to the light spectrum with a "red" and a "violet" pole.

But he soon realized how inadequate that formulation was. For example we now know that physical symptoms in diseases, for example, can

---

[20] Remember Roy G. Biv?—an acronym for the colors of the light spectrum: Red, orange, yellow, green, blue, indigo, violet.

be symbols.[21] I remember a workaholic man who developed a melanoma—in the shape of the state of Florida, communicating to him, with that, what his dreams were saying: relax! So what Jung, along traditional lines, first called instinctual and conservative is not an accurate description of the body's physiological processes. We can no longer say, if we acknowledge that the body conveys symbolic messages, that symbols belong to the mental sphere only: that is not a complete understanding of them. They are not simply mental images. Symbols also belong to the instinctual sphere, the life of the body. And symbols can also appear in the outer material world in the form of a synchronicity.

So Jung soon realized that he could not limit images to a separate existence apart from the body and its instincts, and from matter. The two poles which he first described as separate dynamisms really overlap. Another way to say it is that the image-producing capacity of the personality is not limited to the inner psychological world only. Put in a broader way, the unconscious, the world of dream images, is not limited to our inner psychology. This is essential to grasp. Human psychology is not only something intangible; it also exists in our body and in the matter of the outer world. Jung saw that the aspects of life usually called separate—inner mental and emotional, and outer material and physical—share a secret symmetry. Psychology and physics appropriate a common ground.

Jung's reflections include one more term: the archetype. The archetype is the factor that creates images in dreams and shapes the character of our conscious experience. It is the image-shaping factor within us that arranges our experience and our dream images along certain lines. So previously where I said "image," I could have more precisely said "image-creating factor." I used the word "image" because it is easier to visualize. The archetype was, in Jung's first formulation, thought to be part of our "mental" makeup, one side of our psychological energy, the instinct being the other side of the equation. Archetypes were first thought to be the capacity to create images in our dreams as well as to organize conscious experience, a part of our mental inheritance, with instincts be-

---

[21] As in the work of Anne Maguire and Alfred Ziegler cited above in the introduction.

ing part of our behavioral inheritance. Archetypes, to return to the light simile, were visualized to be on the violet side of the spectrum, instincts on the other red side, opposite the violet. But eventually Jung knew that wouldn't do. Archetypes, as our image-creating capacity, are not separate from our biology nor from matter, since both the body and the material world can act symbolically. Jung coined a word to indicate that archetypes are not merely psychological, and he began referring to the archetype as *psychoid*. By that he meant "psychic-like." Thus Jung expanded his concept of the archetype beyond the inner psychology of the person. The archetype is both inner and outer, mental and physical, psychological and material.

Synchronicity

Von Franz in this first chapter introduces the intersecting of psyche and matter. That leads her to ask if there are parallel structures within psyche and matter. How is it possible that the life of our mind and the life of our body are linked—so much so that at times the body seems to have an intelligence perhaps greater than our mind? Our workaholic fellow refused to admit that he was driven and unbending, but his body didn't. Physical circumstances can depict psychological images often in advance of our conscious understanding. How can the inert, physical world possess intelligence? And what are we supposed to do about it? The link between the two worlds of psyche and matter is expressed most directly and commonly in our lives by synchronistic events.

What is synchronicity?

Von Franz explains:

(Synchronicity) consists of a symbolic image constellated in the psychic inner world, a dream, for instance, or a waking vision, or a sudden hunch originating in the unconscious, which coincides in a "miraculous" manner, not causally or rationally explicable, with an event of similar meaning in the outer world.[22] [6]

Some examples are in order. First I will describe a synchronistic event

---

[22] Page references to *Number and Time* are in brackets following a quoted passage.

of my own when I was in training at the Jung Institute in Zürich. In this case the meaningful coincidence was between an inner state of mind and an outer event. Then I will describe a synchronicity experienced by an analysand where the meaningful coincidence was between a dream image and an outer event.

My initial years of training in Zürich were difficult. The first analyst I chose was not right for me. I could only find a crummy place to live. The value of the dollar dropped, and I was going more in debt than reason would allow. Nevertheless, after an exploratory year, I wanted to remain in Switzerland, but my partner did not. She returned to the United States, ending the relationship. So I pursued my studies at the cost of something very dear. It seemed, however, that my fortunes would be turning when I received a scholarship grant from Rotary International. It was a full year's tuition and living expenses, to be given in two half-year installments. The first installment was paid at the beginning of the fall semester, the second installment was to be paid half way through the year, that is, at the beginning of the winter/spring semester and after a substantial amount of paperwork was completed. At the beginning of the fall semester that year I had my eight midpoint oral qualifying exams—shortly after I had received the first payment. Everything turned wrong again, it seemed, when the one exam where I most respected the examiner, who was Marie-Louise von Franz, found me failing miserably. Not only did I flub gruesomely, but she started banging on the table as I continued to give wrong answer after wrong answer. This was more than a little unnerving. I don't think she was as angry as she was frustrated that I was not coming out with what I knew. She failed me in no uncertain terms. So I left that exam room feeling very low, and I said to myself, "I quit." I felt that everything was indicating to me that I should "go home."

By the exit of the Institute was a shelf where students could pick up their mail, and as I was leaving I saw an envelope addressed to me on the top of a pile of about forty letters. So I grabbed it as I stomped out, opening it on the way down the stairs. I was flabbergasted. Inside it was the second Rotary check. That check was paid six months in advance without my having filled out any of the paperwork. It was sitting neatly on top of a pile of letters, a pile usually in disarray as students scrambled for some news from home. I couldn't avoid the message: "Don't give up."[23]

The synchronicity consisted in the fact that there was, inside of me, a strong emotion of self-doubt, despair really, and then there was a response to that inner state from the outer world. The convergence of the inner and outer, the apparently meaningful action of an outer world event, the fact that it can convey information just like a dream, is what impressed Jung. It is why he extended his recognition of the image-creating factor, originally conceived as a purely psychological affair, to be somehow connected with outer, material reality.

Another example of a synchronicity shows a meaningful coincidence between a dream image and an outer event. A man in the second half of life dreamed:

> I am looking at a small white house from the side. There is a fenced area on this side of the house that runs from front to the back of the house. The grass is very green. In the fenced yard area is a beautiful horse. It is owned by a Black couple, and I am told it is a champion. The horse's name is Havercock.

Here are the dreamer's comments:

> Black couples do not typically own champion horses. The name Haver-cock is unusual, and I have no conscious memory of encountering that name. I Googled the name on the Internet and . . . followed that lead to a restaurant in Tuscany in the town of Montalcino. The principal chef at an apparently famous restaurant is Guido Havercock. The restaurant is in a very old castle in this ancient town in Tuscany.
>
> Eight days after this dream occurred I was in Barnes and Noble. As I was working my way out of the store, I stopped at several display tables to look at books on display. I wasn't looking for anything in particular. On the last table I stopped at there was a book, *A Vineyard in Tuscany: a Wine Lover's Dream* by Ferenc Máté. He and his family live in a thirteenth-century friary in Montalcino, Tuscany. Yes, I purchased the book.

The book is an account of the author's purchase of a thirteenth-century

---

[23] I retook the exam a semester later and recouped my honor.

friary in Montalcino and his successful struggle to fashion the land into a vineyard producing robust harvests of grapes.[24]

The synchronistic event of finding the book at Barnes and Noble extended the dream image of the horse named "Havercock," through the town of Montalcino, to be connected with a winery. The meaning of the horse "Havercock" is not at all clear from the dream, but its meaning unravels in the outer "coincidence" to be connected thematically with the production of wine.

The horse would represent a certain quantity of energy in the dreamer which can carry him through the second half of his life. He associated to African-Americans, the owners of the horse, that African-Americans have had to, and still have to, struggle to attain their place in life. This would mean that the completion of the dreamer's life will involve facing struggle, though the green field would suggest that the struggle will bring fertility and growth. The dreamer rejected a sexual interpretation of "Havercock"—saying sex, in itself, had never been a problem. The place where he felt he did suffer over "masculine potency" was in the area of creativity. The dreamer was asking himself how he could continue to live meaningfully through to the end of life. He felt the phallic implication in the word "Havercock" referred to a *cultural* potency, a *cultural* creativity, masculine potency in that generative sense.

This is reflected in the winery image appended to the dream by the synchronicity at Barnes and Noble. Jung interprets wine to represent culture, since societies in human history that have had the leisure to produce wine, a labor-intensive product, have also had the leisure for artists and artisans to produce art and other cultural artifacts. Thus Jung sees wine

---

[24] From *Publishers Weekly*, cited on Amazon.com: "Máté recounts in wry, candid detail how he rebuilt a Tuscan ruin into a world-class winery. Living in Tuscany with his artist wife and son while savoring the landscape, food and pleasant neighbors wasn't enough for Máté, who admits he thrives on adversity. He wanted his own castle and finagles the purchase of a 13th-century friary in Montalcino, with . . . 60 acres of land—15 of which he fashions over three hard years of work into a vineyard sprouting robust harvests of Sangiovese, Merlot, Cabernet Sauvignon and Syrah grapes. . . . While hacking in the forest, he finds the remains of a 3,000-year-old city, inviting the interest of archeologists." [edited for brevity] (Amazon.com, "*A Vineyard in Tuscany: A Wine Lover's Dream*")

symbolically to "represent a definite cultural achievement which is the fruit of attention, patience, industry, devotion, and laborious toil."[25]

The dreamer was being prompted, both from inner feelings and from other dreams, to write and speak publicly about certain controversial cultural issues of our time. This work would be the "phallic" generativity which is alluded to in the horse's name and which would continue to make the dreamer's life meaningful. This is the "wine" he is to make— even at the cost of the adversity it will bring into his life (seen in his association to African-Americans and evidenced in the struggle, described by the author of the book, to create the vineyard in Montalcino).

Whereas the first synchronicity I described consisted in the parallelism of an inner state of mind and an outer event, the Havercock dream shows how a synchronicity can be the coincidence between an inner dream image and an outer event. Consistent between the two examples is the convergence of inner and outer which impressed Jung so much and which forms the background of von Franz's inquiry.

The I Ching

Synchronicity is one type of experience that led Jung to a broader understanding of the archetype. The I Ching is another:

> At the time that Jung began to observe more closely this type of phenomenon [synchronicity], he became acquainted with the Sinologist Richard Wilhelm who introduced him to the deeper ideas of the ancient Chinese book of oracles and wisdom, the I Ching. [6]

The I Ching is an oracle thought to be about 6,000 years old.[26] Richard Wilhelm was a German Protestant missionary to China, a true lover of Chinese culture not a proselytizer of Western values. Providing the first competent interpretation of the I Ching for Westerners, he was just the man to give Jung valuable access to this text.

---

[25] C.G. Jung, "Transformation Symbolism in the Mass," *Psychology and Religion,* CW 11, pars. 382f.

[26] See Richard Wilhelm, trans., *The I Ching or Book of Changes*, rendered into English by Cary F. Baynes; also C.G. Jung, *Memories, Dreams, Reflections*, p. 373n.

There are a couple of methods to query the I Ching. I learned the "coin" method. One throws three coins six times, and from the numerical results one of 64 patterns is constructed. Consulting the commentary for the particular pattern provides the response to a question and thus makes up the oracular reply from the I Ching. In a sense this oracular procedure is trying to "create" a synchronicity. Whereas a synchronicity is the appearance in material reality of an inner psychological pattern, the ancient Chinese view held that by intentionally creating a certain situation in physical reality, the generation of a numbered pattern through the repeated tossing of coins, one could "read" the inner psychological significance of a particular situation in life. In a synchronicity an image appears in a real situation, and in the I Ching a real situation is created by "chance" throws which express an image that in turn reflects and gives insight into an inner and outer psychological state. Both synchronistic events and the oracular I Ching substantiated the necessity of Jung's widening view of the archetype. Both of these phenomena are important to *Number and Time.* Von Franz refers to them repeatedly as examples of where the inner and outer worlds meaningfully join as a material event in the "outer" world conveys a message for the significance of our lives.

The *Unus Mundus*

We have looked at the comparable views and overlapping subject matter of Jung's psychology and the new physics. We have seen how Jung widened his archetypal hypothesis to include body and matter, and we touched on the two kinds of experiences that prompted him to see the equivalence of psyche and matter. Now the deeper significance of these points is discussed:

> Insofar as similar structures manifest themselves through synchronistic phenomena both in the unconscious psyche *and* in matter, the unity of existence . . . which underlies the duality of psyche and matter becomes more comprehensible to us. Jung applied the term *unus mundus* to this aspect of the unity of existence. [8]

In the final analysis the idea of the *unus mundus* is founded, as Jung says, on the assumption that the multiplicity of the empirical world rests on an underlying unity, and that not two or more fundamentally different worlds exist side by side or are mingled with one other. Rather, everything divided and different belongs to one and the same world, which is not the world of sense but a postulate.[27] [9]

With these passages von Franz and Jung are preparing the way for an important perspective on life which inevitably comes out of the serious study of dreams. Events in life which appear random—a divorce, a bankruptcy, bad experiences, for example—can at times be part of the unfolding and fulfillment of the larger meaning of our lives, painful but necessary events on the way to deeper fulfillment. So if there is a crisis in life, analytic work tries to understand how the mess can be a kind of hidden contribution to our larger development. The appearance of synchronistic events within these times of trial—as indicated by both of the examples I just mentioned—suggest a depth to the suffering waiting to be grasped.

Let's look at the above passages to understand this more fully. "Similar structures" means that an event that happens in time and space can be a reflection of an image in the unconscious. So the "similar structure" is the image in the unconscious and then the presence of that image manifesting in reality. Recall the image chain: Havercock, Tuscany, winery. There is an inner image (Havercock) and the outer event (the book at Barnes and Noble describing the area where Guido Havercock worked, eventually leading to the winery—the construction of which reflected the same adversity the dreamer associated to African-Americans). That is what she means by "similar structures." When Jung saw that kind of thing he asked himself, "Where do dreams occur?" The dream at times seems to occur in outer reality. Both dream and outer reality reflect the same image, the same structure.

Now consider the phrase "on the assumption that the multiplicity of the empirical world"—that is, outer events—"rests on an underlying unity." That unity is seen in the similarity between the inner images or states of mind, and their duplicate appearance in the outer world. So the question arises, *is there some "one thing" that these two appearances*

---

[27] *Mysterium Coniunctionis,* CW 14, par. 767.

are different aspects of? It is not likely simply the case that there is a mere coincidence between inside and outside, but that inside and outside, in their appearing to work in tandem at certain moments, hint that they could be two sides of something bigger, a unity that we habitually experience in two parts. That is what is meant by "not two or more fundamentally different worlds exist side by side or are mingled with one other." If there is a unity of those apparently different worlds, what is that something bigger? Well, we don't know in any certain way. But this book attempts to circumscribe just what that "higher" unity that appears in two seemingly separate places in our lives, inside and outside, might be. Hence the statement: "Everything divided and different belongs to one and the same world."

Von Franz resumes: "Jung stresses, however, that there is little or no hope of illuminating this undivided existence except through antinomies." [9]

Antinomies are contradictions. What are the antinomies here? They are the two different ways of looking at life, from the inner psychological and outer physical points of view. Those two make up one world, but that world can't be explained solely as one world, it has to be explained as two parts of one world. So ironically we are talking about a unity, but the only way that unity can be described is through a duality. We will be shuttling back and forth between the two ways this possible unity manifests, in the inner world and in the outer world. But we will always be cognizant of the fact that we are looking at two sides of a whole, however a whole that is beyond the grasp of rational cognition though we may very well have a feeling sense of its singleness.

Whenever Jung discerned something about human nature or a life-process which is not readily accepted in our current manner of looking at life, he cast around in the past to see if anyone else had had similar experiences and if anyone else had given expression to what he had just seen. He soon recognized that medieval alchemists had described a unity to existence, a unity that exists between two normally separated parts of experience—the mental or psychological side of life and the physical, material world—in their term *unus mundus*, that is, one world.

They used this term in two senses. First they thought there was a harmonious plan for all of life, existing as a potential to be realized. Of course, this is medieval, pre-scientific thinking. Remember that alchemists were pre-chemists who worked in their laboratories trying to turn some worthless piece of material into gold or other valuable substance. Describing by means of a symbolic language what was going on in their supposed transforming substance, they made use of the same language that dreams do. Jung studied their work as a metaphor for the psychological transformation within individuals who undertake a personal journey. What the alchemists thought was a process of change in matter, Jung understood symbolically as an inner, psychological process of transformation within us.

So, as I said, these alchemists thought that the world as a harmonious spiritual-physical whole existed in potential. They also thought that, when they were working in their alchemical laboratories, they not only could turn the chaos of the base material they were working on into a harmony as the gold was produced, but that, after the harmony was established within their alchemical vessel, it could have a beneficent effect on the world and induce "out there" what had been produced in the "in here" of their vessel. That moment when harmonious contents of the vessel induced a harmony in the outer world they likewise called the *unus mundus*. So the *unus mundus* in the medieval mind was the potential for harmony between the spiritual and the material as well as the evoking of harmony from within their transformed substance to bring the outside world into that harmonious state. Jung simply adopted that word to denote the possibility that behind the parallelism of images inside and outside of us there is a potential for unity that is surfacing on two sides. This is a hypothesis, and that is why he calls it a postulate—not something that can be proved. It is inferred to exist from the fact that synchronistic moments unite two sides of life, our "insides" and our "outsides" in a single image.

The Transcendental Continuum

The plot thickens:

> But we do know for certain *that the empirical world of appearances is in some way based on a transcendental background.* It is *this* background which, suddenly as it were, falls into our conscious world through synchronistic happenings. [9]

There are two important notions here: the "transcendental background" and "falls in." Soon we will see another, the relation of the "transcendental background" and "falls in" to "number."

First, the transcendental background needs explication. In doing this, von Franz turns to a seventeenth-century Chinese philosopher, Wang Fu Ch'ih:

> He made an attempt to clarify the mysterious working of the Book of Changes, the I Ching, from the philosophical point of view. According to Wang Fu Ch'ih's interpretation, all existence is finally based on *an all-containing continuum which is itself lawfully ordered* but which "in itself … is without perceptual manifestation" and is therefore not immediately accessible to sensory perception. [10]

The transcendental background, intuited by Jung and here discussed in early Chinese philosophy, is a key ingredient in Jung's view. As I suggested in the introduction, he holds that we are born who we are—identity, for Jung, being inborn. He writes in one place of "the individual ground-plan" and in another of "the basic blueprint."[28] This given identity is not something normally completely and immediately available to our conscious experience. But it does exist, although apart, often seemingly distant from the vicissitudes of daily life. When we look at our lives up close, it can seem that they are made up of one chaotic event after the other. But with the view of time, and certainly by examining dream images and looking at our lives through them, we can get a sense that there is a larger pattern trying to come to fruition in our life through

---

[28] See *Aion*, CW 9ii, par. 297; also Lorenz Jung and Maria Meyer-Grass, eds., *Children's Dreams: Notes from the Seminar*, p. 20.

its ups and downs. Since this pattern is not immediately obvious, and can often at best be merely intuited or inferred, Jung calls it transcendental, that is, beyond our normal capacity for direct perception.[29] The story of our life does already exist in potential, and is pushing to come into being, though we only get glimpses of it bit by bit. Hence:

> In Wang Fu Ch'ih's view the dynamism inherent in this universal continuum differentiates certain images which, in their structure and position, participate in the conformity of the continuum. Since these images are *in themselves ordered and therefore lawful, they participate in the world of number and can be grasped in a numerical procedure.* In other words, they . . . [are] numerically structured. These images can of course also be grasped directly, emotionally and experientially, without the benefit of an arithmetical procedure. But number opens up a theoretical and speculative method of approaching the situations represented by such images. [10]

"An all-containing continuum" is a reference to the transcendental background. "Which is itself lawfully ordered" means the transcendental background is a continuum. It holds the sequential unfolding of our life's continuous story in a way that is ordered; it is not random. Events in time and space lived unconsciously are random. But in the realm of the pre-existent possibility, the ground-plan or blueprint, our life has the potential to go from stage one to stage two to stage three to stage four to stage five, and so on. In time and space life is chaos—until the transcendental continuum pattern seeks to manifest, apparently from an impulsion within itself. So at certain moments what needs to be understood in a particular phase of our life "drops down," and a synchronicity occurs. If we understand it, we have the possibility of reorienting our life. In my synchronicity example, staying in Zürich and completing my training was part of the basic plan of my life. Hence the synchronistic event "intervened" with that message. In the case of the dreamer, creative and cultural accomplishment belongs to his story, so the synchronicity presented a little piece of it to him in his dream and at Barnes and Noble. When it is time for the next stage of our life to occur, an image of that potentiality

---

[29] Von Franz stipulates that she is using this word to mean "transcending consciousness." It does not necessarily imply a metaphysical reference.

"drops down," into reality as a synchronicity for the purpose of educating us how life wants to develop.

The entirety of the transcendental background or continuum, the quote from the Chinese philosopher goes on to say, is not directly available to experience. It is only in dreams and in synchronicities, when the transcendental possibilities of our life clothe themselves in those experiences materially available to us, that it can be perceived. So these dream images and synchronicities, when they are recognized, digested, and acted on, bring a direction to the otherwise chaotic-seeming events and happenings in life. This is how the transcendental realm of possibilities—which exists in the form of images pregnant with life—enters into time and space.[30]

Numbers

Now we come to numbers. "Differentiates certain images" means, as I have said, that the potential in the transcendental continuum enters into daily life at certain moments. The image becomes separate from the largely directly unknowable continuum and crystallizes into a real event. The next part of the passage brings us to part of the title of the book:

> Since these images are in themselves ordered and therefore lawful, they participate in the world of number. [10]

The "ordered" refers to there being a *first*, a *second*, a *third* stage of life, etc. In saying that I have just used numbers to express the evolution of my development. That means there is something of a numerical structure to this potential world. Where there is sequence there is number. So the sense of meaningful order in our everyday life in time and space comes from the transcendental continuum becoming manifest and reorienting our life toward its genuine unfolding—in a relatively sequential way.

---

[30] I have often been asked, when discussing this material in workshops, "What happens if I miss it?" I do think there are second chances, but a limited number of them. We don't get ten chances. The discussion here presupposes an ego that can register and understand what it is experiencing.

The transcendental dimension becoming real through our recognizing and responding to its message is, by its very nature, an ordering experience, in the sense of creating meaningful development of our life's progress.

The quote above continues in the book with reference to "numerical procedures" which suggests the oracular techniques she discusses in chapter 12. For the moment notice how the discussion has evolved from meaning to sequence and numbers. Hence *Number and Time* will attempt to understand, from the way numbers appear in dreams, mythology, mathematics, and physics, how they can be symbols of life's most significant processes and how they can be a bridge to help us to appreciate those moments of life when matter operates symbolically.

Chapter Summary

Synchronistic events, with their evidencing the unity of a "one world," are in Jung's words "acts of creation in time."[31] With his investigation into these particular moments, Jung has shown us not only another example of the human personality's capacity to reorient itself, to heal and to grow, he has also presented for our consideration an entirely new conception of creative forces appearing inside and outside ourselves which reside we know not where.

---

[31] *Number and Time,* pp. 230, 254.

Chapter 2

Images and Mathematical Structures in Relation to the *Unus Mundus*

In chapter 2 von Franz establishes that numbers and the unconscious have a very tight connection. When we first look at a number dream or we have a dream in which we are in a math class or in an algebra class, our first reaction may be that the dream is about our being too rational or "in our head" or something like that. But, as we will see, numbers are not "rational" at all. Particularly in the dream world they represent not quantities but qualities. To substantiate that point she will discuss examples of scientific and mathematical discoveries that came from dreams or sudden inspirations, where the conclusion wasn't thought out but was recognized in a flash.

Why is she doing this? To show us that numbers aren't things that merely originate in rational thought. They are just as much images with a connection to the unconscious as anything in mythology. Thus we are justified in discussing them, not as clear and logical entities, not as counting units, but as representative of inner processes, symbolically as rich as an image of Zeus or Aphrodite, Gilgamesh or Ishtar.

Numbers and the Big Picture

On page 15 von Franz reviews Jung's observation that when the conscious mind reaches a block the unconscious becomes active and responds with images that point the way through the stoppage. When we are in the dark and perplexed over something, the unconscious mind can be counted on to generate an image in dreams or waking fantasies which points to an answer that the conscious mind could not have conceived of on its own. She mentions that because she wants to recognize what the unconscious mind at the deeper level has come up with as a way of comprehending this unity of existence which is two. How has the psyche of humankind expressed the enigma of totality?

38

She mentions several examples: Wang Fu Ch'ih, Einstein, quantum physics, and Niels Bohr.[32] The common element in all the models of the universe put forward by these sources is that they see numbers, a geometric continuum, to be the final reality. In their attempts to conceptualize and describe a working model for the nature of the universe, they all end up with a numerical description—one way or the other. The exact extent of their descriptions need not occupy us in a first attempt to appreciate this book, but a particular feature common to their models of reality is important to von Franz's developing point of view. In the final analysis, the sources she cites cannot describe the nature of reality without reference to mathematical structures. In other words, as soon as the creative mind seeks to understand the totality of what is, numbers appear as a response to the inquiry.

So the answer to how the psyche expresses the notion of totality is that it cannot do so without recourse to number and geometric models. We are to concede, thereby, that numbers are not merely counting units. They belong to the very fiber of the human imagination and its seeking to express the mystery of the way the world works.

Numbers and the Unconscious

Von Franz cites Wolfgang Pauli[33] in this vein to express the importance of numbers in our imagination and dream life. Numbers should be considered as archetypes:

---

[32] We'll see more of Bohr and quantum mechanics in the next chapter, and Einstein's universe will reappear in chapter 7.

[33] Wolfgang Pauli was one of the discoverers of quantum physics in Copenhagen in 1927. Taking up the chair of physics at the technical university in Zürich in 1928, he was active in Jungian psychology for the rest of his life, a charter member of the board ("Curatorium") of the first C.G. Jung Institute. His initial contact with Jung was shortly after he arrived in Zürich and was going through a painful divorce as well as the suicide of his mother. During the years in Zürich he maintained personal and professional relationships with Jung and a variety of other Jungians, among them Marie-Louse von Franz and Aniela Jaffé. He consulted Jung again after World War Two to process his dreams concerning the horrors of the war and its atomic end. Those dreams, often dealing with the relationship between psyche and matter, have been published throughout the Jungian literature. For more on him see my book *At the Heart of Matter*.

Wolfgang Pauli postulated that the "basic intuitions" of mathematics, the idea of an infinite series of whole numbers, for instance . . . should be included in Jung's concept of archetypal ideas. [18]

Saying that numbers are archetypes means, again, that they are fundamental constituents of our imagination. Just as we have learned to pay particular attention to mythological images in our interpretation of dreams because they express psychological characteristics and emotional conditions of critical importance to our health and wellbeing, so now we can also identify the same symbolic power in numbers. Insofar as "mathematical structures rest on an archetypal basis" and likewise insofar as "archetypes engender images and ideas," [19] acknowledging the archetypal character of number allows the creative imagination of the dream an important avenue for expression. Another dimension of symbolic understanding and its potency thus becomes available for us.

I remember the first time the symbolic, qualitative aspect of number in dreams was driven forcibly home to me. As a trainee in Zürich I was working with a woman who complained continually about her husband. He was in fact at that time having an affair. And after talking with her for a while I started feeling that I didn't blame him. She was an enormously unpleasant person. In the context of our analytic work she dreamed that she and her husband were looking for a new apartment. They went into a building where an apartment was available on the third floor and another on the fourth floor. The apartment on the third floor was bathed in light, everything was cheery and bright. The apartment on the fourth floor was a mixture of light and dark, sun streaming in and shadowed spots. She, in the dream, wanted the third floor apartment, he the fourth floor apartment. They went to marriage counseling for a bit, and later I talked to the marriage counselor who, true to what was revealed in the dream, told me that the woman would not deal with any dark feelings whatsoever. They finally divorced. The dream contained the number four, the wholeness number, as we will see,[34] and it was he who really wanted to have a relationship with good days and bad days, where the complexity of emotion

---

[34] Chapter 7 will discuss the symbolism of the number four, and chapter 6 will consider the psychological importance of the number three.

could live, whereas she wanted everything bright and sunny all the time—more characteristic of the psychology of the number three. That, for me, was a striking example of how numbers show up as qualitative indicators with rich unconscious content. By coincidence, I met the couple's youngish children at a social event in Switzerland during this time, and it was very painful to see the suffering they were enduring as a result of the parents' divorce. All of that was contained in the little detail of the numbers three and four. Those dream images conveyed a weight of emotional meaning, with effects on the lives of two people and their children.

In order to continue helping us grasp just how numbers belong to the unconscious sphere, von Franz turns to scientific and mathematical discoveries that have come out of dreams or have come in a sudden flash of insight. She discusses [20-22] the mathematical discoveries of Henri Poincaré, Karl Friedrich Gauss, Felix Klein, and Descartes. She also turns to China to illustrate how certain meaningful number patterns were said to have been magically "given." The I Ching's origin is reputed to have come into being similarly. These various examples show from their vantage points how numbers and the unconscious have a connection. The specific mathematical discoveries don't have to bog us down if we are not arithmetically minded, but the general idea of the relation of numbers to unconscious creation in mathematics and science is the important point to remember.

Since this is such a new idea for most of us it bears repeating: numbers aren't just rational things. Numbers share an intimate relation to non-rational creative unconscious processes; numbers are qualitative expressions of our inner nature. They originate "from the deepest levels of the collective unconscious." [26]

Numbers Regulate

Thus far the importance of numbers as representing the sequential unfolding of our life's story and, similarly, their affinity to the processes of the unconscious in general has occupied the discussion. Von Franz now introduces a perspective on numbers which she will develop in the next chapter, a perspective which forms the backbone of her work:

Natural integers contain the very element which regulates the unitary realm of psyche and matter. It will also substantiate his [Jung's] contention that number serves as a special instrument for becoming conscious of such unitary patterns. [27]

To recognize the importance of number in this regard means, of course:

Our concept of number must first be broadened in several respects before we can apply it to the investigation of synchronicity. [28]

This naturally has been her point in the present chapter—that we begin to enlarge our perception of numbers to include their qualitative, non-rational aspect since, in the dream life of the unconscious, they appear and function as highly pregnant symbols imbued with particular significance. She will turn to further discussion of that emotional significance in the chapter after next. But in the immediately following chapter 3, the nature of the unitary realm of psyche and matter takes precedence. We have seen, to some extent, the role of numbers in the psychological realm.[35] But what is their pertinence to matter? She will next draw our attention to the connection between numbers and the material world. It is, she stresses, this connection between the numerical construction of matter and the role of numbers in our life's story—the successive stages of life's development being a built-in feature of meaning—which creates the bridge between matter and spirit.[36] And it is that bridge which, in a synchronistic moment, fills otherwise dull matter with its living impact, so that she fittingly brings the chapter to a close with this:

It is not what we can *do* with numbers but what *they* do to our consciousness that is essential. [33]

---

[35] We will see more in chapters 4, 5, and 6.
[36] She will define "spirit" in the next chapter.

Chapter 3

Number as the Basic Manifestation of the Mind and As the Unalterable Quality of Matter

Chapter 3 discusses number as an aspect of the psyche and of matter, the shared characteristic which unites them and establishes meaning. This insight sums up part I.

Yikes, More Physics!

We have touched on how quantum physics shares a common insight with Jungian psychology concerning of the limits of causality as a principle of nature. In order to grasp her contention that number is what unites psyche and matter, it will be useful briefly to return to science again to see how quantum physics, in its recognition of the building block of material reality, the atom, enters into the discussion once more.

In 1900 Max Planck discovered in tangential laboratory research that energy only exists in discrete units. Energy is not something that can have any value; it can only exist in very teensy, specified values. In big interactions in our everyday experience, that value is so small that it looks and feels like energy goes up and down on a sliding scale. It feels like the thermometer rises slowly and continuously as the day gets warmer but really it is going up in very small jumps; it is just that the size of those jumps is too small for us to notice. However, those jumps are noticeable in the minute world of subatomic particles. There is no reason that this should be so. It just is that way. "Planck's Constant" is the term given for that very small energy gradation which can exist only in whole number multiples.

Just as there are only discrete energy levels allowed to physical energy, so likewise there are only discrete energy levels allowed to the electron orbits in the atom. Again, there is no reason for that; it is just the way they are. The quantum physicists—among them Jung's future friend Wolfgang Pauli—gathered around Niels Bohr in Copenhagen figured this out in the years through 1927 by investigating the bands of light (spectra) emitted by glowing gasses. Nothing in classical physics can explain or could have anticipated the "just so" nature of energy and electron orbits in the atom. Quantum physics can't explain it either, so it gave up trying to explain and became satisfied with merely describing. Nature has some built-in numerical forms, period. And the new physics mathematically describes how they work and interact.

Why is this noteworthy for us?

Numbers Unite

Nature, as the psyche, is numerically structured. There is an inherent form to processes at the microlevel in nature. Nature is not completely random. Nature has a shape and a structure in this "just so" fashion. The psyche, we have seen, is not random either. The sequential unfolding of life, like the built-in value of Planck's constant, is inherent. Meaning and sequence are very closely related. When we can no longer feel our life has gone first from one stage, through another stage, and onto a third stage, and so on, we are in trouble. Then despair sets in. Why is life like that? It is the "just so" of the human condition. That there is a structure both to the psyche—the nature of our life-story—and to matter—the discrete energy level for the electron, for example[37]—is what unites them.

In Jung's words:

> Matter and spirit both appear in the psychic realm as distinctive qualities of conscious contents. The ultimate nature of both is transcendental, that is, irrepresentational, since the psyche and its contents are the only reality which is imparted directly to us.[38] [37]

Von Franz comments:

> According to Jung, number appears to display an exact relation to *both*

---

[37] There are others: for instance the "just so" nature of the decay rate of radioactive elements; the incredibly beautiful and consistent patterns of the shape of the electron orbits around the nucleus of the atom such as is figured on page 49 of *Number and Time*.

[38] "On the Nature of the Psyche," *The Structure and Dynamics of the Psyche*, CW 8, par. 420.

spheres. Number forms not only an essential aspect of every material manifestation but is just as much a product of the mind (meaning the dynamic aspect of the unconscious psyche).[39] It appears in our mental processes as a purely archetypal preconscious basic structure. [37]

In the previous two chapters she considered number's role in the psychological realm. Here she is bringing particular attention to the fact that number is also a quality of matter; she is stressing how both the psyche and matter share a unity in number. Matter and psyche are two sides of the same thing. Numbers evidence in what way matter and psyche are essentially a unity; though matter and psyche share that unity, we perceive them as separate in our day-to-day reality.

Thus she recaps later in the chapter:

Numbers appear to represent both an attribute of matter and the unconscious foundation of our mental processes. For this reason, number forms, according to Jung, that particular element that unites the realms of matter and psyche. [52]

This conception of number presupposes, as we have recognized of course, that we can see numbers outside of our "arithmetic" experience of them. Their fundamental nature is qualitative. This she discusses from pages 31 through 41.

A story von Franz tells puts the point at its most charming:

There were eleven [Chinese] generals, and they had to vote if they should attack or retreat. They voted, and eight were for attack and three were for going back. Therefore, they retreated. The three had won out because three is a number of harmony; three is a better number, qualitatively, than eight. The people who hit the three won out.[40]

---

[39] There is a subtlety here in the German lost to English readers. The German word *Geist* means both spirit and mind. The original use of the word referred to the mind as that capacity to perceive and assess spirit. Since the Scientific Revolution and the Enlightenment, the word *Geist* has come increasingly to mean the mind as the capacity to perceive and rationally manipulate data. Its original spiritual function has been completely lost. Her parenthetic comment refers back to that original meaning of the word as what can give shape to life through its apprehension of the winds of personal (and societal) change. See Jung, *Nietzsche's Zarathustra,* pp. 378ff.

[40] *Psyche and Matter,* p. 164.

Which Time Is It?

Time, the other word in the title of her book, now enters the discussion.

> This time-bound aspect of number is closely connected with the general outlook of early Chinese thought, which was oriented to the principle of synchronicity instead of causality. It is therefore worth [outlining] the basic difference between our causal and their synchronistic mode of thought. [42]

Von Franz then explicates that idea which we may profitably sum up with reference to the synchronicities I mentioned in chapter 1. Synchronicity, this link between psyche and matter, is the convergence of the psychological plan of our life's story with a material event in reality which reflects in a symbolic image what we need to know to further our life's development—recall the letter which "said," "don't give up" to my doubt, the book at Barnes and Noble which "said" to the dreamer's confusion, "cultural creation is your next task." The union of inner state and outer event, she has held, is made possible by the unity of their shared numerical structure. But that unity of the outer world acting symbolically in consort with an inner state or image only manifests *at certain moments*. Those moments are special moments; they are moments of a particular *qualitative* weight for our maturation. *That* day was the day to know not to give up. What if receiving the letter had occurred on a different day? It would not have had its impact. *That* moment of the dreamer's life was the important one for him to make certain decisions to get his life back on track. Why did the dream and synchronicity occur to the dreamer in the time it did? Because he was asking the right question: what shall I do *now*?

Accordingly, number cannot be divorced from time because these synchronistic events, made possible by the numerical similarity of psyche and matter, occur at the *right moment*. It is as if "they" know of the quality of the particular moment of life in which they occur, and they reflect that to us if we are willing and able to listen. Not all moments in life are the same; there is a qualitative dimension to time lost normally to Western consciousness. This quality comes to the fore in synchronistic experiences made possible by the comparable numerical nature of outer reality and inner psyche.

It is not a new idea by now, but one given more emotional weight by the recognition of the qualitative aspect of time, when Jung observes thus:

> We define number psychologically as an *archetype of order which has become conscious.*[41] [45]

That "order" or "meaning" is reflected in the qualitative moment of time in which a synchronicity occurs, as if that quality is "known" within the event and its numerical background—in some fashion independent of and prior to our consciously registering it.

Spirit

Pages 46 to 51 examine other examples of the numerical structure of matter which I have described in my one example drawn from physics which may suffice for now for the first-time reader of the book. But within those pages she does introduce a new aspect to her discussion that cannot be skimmed over:

> It is evident that number really represents an unalterable quality of matter, both as a quantitative factor and as the form (and thus a qualitative structure) of an *effective* factor of orderedness. [50, emphasis added]

The word that we will now investigate, and which I have italicized, is *effective.* What is this "effectiveness"? There is something, she writes,

> in the unconscious psyche which engenders, autonomously manipulates, and orders inner images. Number is, as it were, the most accessible primitive manifestation of this transcendental spontaneous principle of movement in the psyche. [53]

This "transcendental principle of movement in the psyche" is what Jung calls spirit. Later in the book von Franz gives another, perhaps more reader-friendly definition of spirit. Spirit is

---

[41] "Synchronicity," *The Structure and Dynamics of the Psyche,* CW 8, par. 870, von Franz's emphasis.

that factor which creates images in the inner field of vision and organizes them into a meaningful order. [214]

It will be clear to anyone who is involved in an exploration of his or her dream processes how dreams evolve as they are understood. When a particular dream is digested, the next dream portrays the issue worked out in the previous dream in a more detailed and deeper fashion, often showing new possibilities for life's development, fresh avenues for growth and fulfillment. Jung called the dynamic of this capacity of the psyche to develop forward sequentially the "spirit."[42] That is to say there is an inner "effectiveness" to dreams and the psychological processes they embrace. Likewise this is to say that there is a capacity for psychological "movement" within us—it's just there. This capacity or dynamism is hypothesized to be implicit in the dreams' moving us forward through life, almost as if there is something in us staging the show, as it were: engendering, manipulating ("arranging" might divest the word of the negative connotations it has in English), and ordering images. But already in the way I've formulated the word "spirit," I've betrayed myself!

No, it is not only on the inside, since we know by now how definite images appear outside of us as well. This ordering capacity "of the psyche" is also—what else could one conclude?—an ordering process of matter. Why does the word "transcendental" come into it? Because this ordering capacity is not something immediately available to our experience. We can see the effects of it as images evolve, with the evolving image either appearing in a dream or in an outer event; we can see its effects but we can't see *it* directly . . . it transcends consciousness.

Let me return to the previous quote:

Number is, as it were, the most accessible primitive manifestation of this transcendental principle of movement in the psyche. [53]

In other words, number is not merely to be recognized as what lies behind the unfolding of a meaningful life, nor as merely an inherent aspect of matter in so far as there is a striking geometric regularity of form

---

[42] *Number and Time,* pp. 214f.

to the smallest of atomic activity, nor merely as what allows the inner world of the psyche and the outer world of matter to form a unity. Number is also one of the prime images that express the dynamic, future-creating activity of the psyche as seen in dreams—no, incomplete again: that express the dynamic, future-creating activity as seen in the meaningful unfolding of our imagery whether that imagery appears inside us in dreams or outside us in material, synchronistic events.

Hence she writes that there is a dynamic ordering factor to life "bound up with matter and the psyche":

> Probably it [the ordering factor] operates (precisely in the form of number) in the background of these two regions . . . Most likely number expresses an essential quality of phenomenon, and phenomenon represents an essential quality of the spirit, and it is precisely these facts that let us guess the existence of a unitary reality (*unus mundus*). In the last analysis, the mystery of the *unus mundus* resides in the nature of number. The means by which we experience the hieroglyphs [meaning "symbolic expressions"] of the *unus mundus* is always a numerical value. [54]

With these considerations her discussion of the role of numbers has thus significantly broadened.

Chapter Summary

Each synchronicity is a *unus mundus*. Each time the transcendental continuum (the potential story of our life) drops down into matter (think of the numerically structured atom), what is happening inside us is the same as is happening outside us. The *unus mundus* (the possibility of which lies in the parallel numerical structure of inside and outside) is the momentary condition of wholeness when inner and outer coincide, and the feeling of those moments is one of unity between inner and outer, meaning and matter. In these synchronistic moments life feels "right," because what is inside us is resonant with what is outside us—this is the sense that comes when the synchronistic moment is understood and its relation to our evolving life is comprehended. And the more what we are doing in time and space is a reflection of the inner potential that is in us in this "transcendental" dimension, the more life becomes satisfying; it is the experience of living a meaningful life.[43] There is a dynamic process to life and growth moving our development forward to its completion as image and reality coincide. Number, as well, symbolizes this dynamism; in other words, number is a prime representation of the spirit.

[43] "We had the experience but missed the meaning, | And approach to the meaning restores the experience | In a different form, beyond any meaning | We can assign to happiness." (T.S. Eliot, "Four Quartets," in *The Complete Poems and Plays*, p. 133)

PART II
The Structure of the First Four Integers

Chapter 4

Number as a Time-bound Quality
of the One-Continuum

There are a couple of main points in chapter 4. The first is not difficult. The second is not difficult conceptually but to feel its meaning is crucial. The first point is that numbers have qualities or that numbers have personalities.[44] That is not an assertion new to the book. Now the second: numbers are points of a continuum. The number one qualitatively contains the whole sequence of natural numbers. Put differently, there is a relationship between unity and multiplicity. Von Franz will be discussing how mathematical number theory "mathematically" understands numbers, and then she will examine how those mathematical descriptions of number portray Jung's discovery of the process of emotional integration. To understand that we will again have to think qualitatively rather than quantitatively.

Here are those two points in her words:

> The great problem posed by the application of natural numbers to the understanding of synchronistic phenomena is, as already mentioned, the fact that a qualitative aspect, rarely taken into account in modern Western number theory, must be attributed to them. At the same time, this aspect lends a new character to the concept of a numerical continuum. [59]

The Numerical Continuum

Now the words "numerical continuum." What do they mean?

---

[44] See her citing on page 60 the French mathematician Henri Poincaré (1854-1912): "Every whole [natural] number . . . possesses its own individuality, so to speak; each one of them forms a kind of exception." [The terms "whole" or "natural" number mean, roughly speaking, not a fraction.]

At the same time, this aspect [i.e., the qualitative aspect of number] lends a new character to the concept of a numerical continuum, since every individual numerical form or structure qualitatively represents an indivisible whole. [59]

Each number is representative of some aspect of the whole. This is a point of view held in both Eastern and Western number theory, as we will see. It is a mathematical statement but, for us, the value in it will emerge when we understand that statement qualitatively and symbolically.

This continuum should not, however, only be conceived of as an indivisible whole, but as a continuum in which every individual number represents the continuum in its entirety. [59]

The part represents the whole . . . again a mathematical statement. It is hard to grasp logically for us non-mathematicians. But we are going to focus on its psychological meaning. So here is a dream that illustrates the symbolic relevance of von Franz's mathematical statement.

The dream is from Jung's *Dream Analysis: Notes of the Seminar*. The seminar concerns a case Jung presented in 1928 to a group of interested students. He concentrated on one man's dreams and spent a year discussing thirty of them with the group. The man and his wife were estranged sexually, and he was visiting prostitutes in Eastern Europe when he traveled there on business. The following is one of the very early dreams he had while working with Jung.

The patient says: "It is as if I were seeing a sort of steamroller from a point above. The machine is going and is apparently making a road, forming a particular pattern like a labyrinth." And in the dream he thinks, "That is my analysis"; and then he is in the picture which he has looked at from above. He is standing at the bifurcation of the road in a wood and he does not know which way to go. At first he did not pay much attention to the arabesque the machine was making.[45] (Figure 2)

Jung interpreted the steamroller as the mechanical nature of the man's

---

[45] *Dream Analysis*, p. 97f.

sexuality. In this regard we might recall James Brown's 1970 song, "Sex Machine." The man's sexuality was physiological, mechanical, pleasure-based. It was driving him all over the place.

What interested Jung, though, was the *pattern* that the man's apparently chaotic, promiscuous, and mechanical sexual behavior created. Look at the drawing the man made of his dream. Note how an *ordered* pattern is created. And look where the steamroller leads him. To the center! The man's instinctive, purely libidinous chaos was actually ordered. It was in fact leading him toward his center. Error contains truth.

Figure 2. The arabesque.

The drive to the center means that, through the chaotic living out of his sexuality and working on it in analysis with Jung, the man now has the possibility of finding himself. All those (we can be sure painful) points on the road are part of the path to the center, to self-knowledge and self-fulfillment. That center is the "one." Because it is one point.[46]

Another way of saying it is that the multiplicity of points on the diagram are a part of the way to the unity of the center. Now just extend the argument. That pattern must somehow "know" of the man's journey to the center. He didn't know consciously, certainly not when he was torn about his marriage and his lust in Eastern Europe, certainly not during this early part of his analysis with Jung, that he was coming to himself precisely *through* the lust and heartache. But something in him, in his instincts—that is what he was living out on that chaotic road of life—"knew" the way to the center. There is no longer a separation, so to speak, between the center and the *way* to the center. The unity of the goal is likewise in the multiplicity of the chaos in getting there. If he hadn't been on that chaotic road, would he have ever reached the center of himself? All the "immoral" junk he was going through on that road was relating him to the center, because it is *just that* road that got him there. This is the paradox about psychological suffering. It is often patterned. And this is what von Franz means by saying that the multiplicity contains the unity, and that the unity contains the multiplicity. Jung's analysand could not have skipped any of those steps in his fragmented life, his "multiplicity," or he wouldn't have found where he was going. There is something related to the goal of unity in the confusion of the multiplicity.

Let's go back to the arabesque, the pattern made by the steamroller. Look at any side of the arabesque. There is a back and forth: one, two. There is a numerical pattern of two on the sides, there is a back and forth, a back and forth. The sides are repeatedly traversed. There is not only a relationship between the multiplicity and the unity, there is also a relationship between the duality of movements in that pattern and the unity.

---

[46] In Jungian jargon this is the Self, the central core of the personality with, we might say, an intelligence of its own. We could also say the Self is our inborn individuality *and* the process by which that individuality seeks to be realized in our life.

The two is a particular feature of that picture of getting to the one.

There is another number implied in the arabesque as well. Two is the back and forth movement seen from the edges. But the path is moving *forward* because of the back and forth. That is to say there are three movements that can be identified in the sketch. When we are caught in a conflict, the back and forth is all we usually feel and see. At those moments in our life we will dream of twos. But eventually we will start dreaming of three, because a forward movement of growth emerges out of the two, out of the endured conflict. In the picture, that is the spiral movement which begins from the back and forth and proceeds to the center of the picture. That three represents the progress and growth which takes off through enduring the conflict. Here we see the essence of what Jung discovered in those years after he split with Freud. Consciously endured conflict—conflict recognized and suffered over (when the blaming stops)—generates synthesis. This, Jung could demonstrate, was an inborn capacity of the human being.[47]

Thus we can see that not only is two related to one, that is, two being a part of the process of growth that leads to one/unity, three is also related to two and one since it represents the movement toward unity/ one/resolved conflict when the "two" or conflict stage is endured. Three is the dynamism of the route to the one when we have gone back and forth over and over and over and over a conflict, symbolized as "two."

Look at that arabesque again. Notice there are four points around the center. There is also a four characteristic of the journey. Four, at least in one of its meanings, would represent the extent of what the man is integrating as he winds his way to his center. Four would here stand for the range of what the man is having to go through, the breadth of his personality which he is integrating through his back and forth leading him to his center.[48]

---

[47] That same process of synthesis emerging from conflict is depicted in the Chinese text "The Secret of the Golden Flower," which gave Jung the courage to say the process was cross-cultural, i.e., an intrinsic capacity of human nature. See his *Memories, Dreams, Reflections*, p. 197, and more of this in chapter 6 here.

[48] Chapter 7 will explore the number four in more depth, including the relationship of totality to emotional openness.

At first all the man felt was chaos. That chaos, he soon learned, was made up of questions like, "Should I get divorced, or should I stay in the marriage?" Back and forth, back and forth. One day one feeling, the next day the other. Twoness. Or: "I want to visit desirable prostitutes" and "I want to have a meaningful and complete relationship with my wife."

There is an enormously important implication in the discussion now for the way Jungian analysis is conducted. We try to understand how what looks like chaos or pathology or incompatibilities in an analysand's personality are necessary ingredients for realizing and creating who he or she really is at the center. In the last instance, the difficulties in our life can be identified as the steps necessary for us to reach ourselves.[49] Each "incompatible tendency" is a part of the future whole. Its integration is the meaning of our torment. Its integration is often what keeps us on the path to the greater whole into which all of ourselves will find a place and purpose in a re-centered and stable personality. This is another perspective on what is meant by the intimate relation between "multiplicity" and "unity." We will see more of the practical, therapeutic implications of this in chapters 8 and 9. For the present moment, the main point is to appreciate the importance of number symbolism in representing all phases of the continuous synthesizing process that leads to the goal.

Von Franz has put the previous discussion in one concise paragraph:

> One comprises wholeness, two divides, repeats, and engenders symmetries [the back and forth in the steamroller picture], three centers the symmetries and initiates linear succession [the movement to the center], four acts as a stabilizer by turning back to the one. [74]

East and West

This recognition of the quality of one is found both in the East and West. Consider von Franz's references to China:

---

[49] Certainly the Jungian approach sees the relevance of returning to the past to uncover the source of the fragmented parts, those personality tendencies that are at odds with each other; but not raising the question of the purpose of the parts and how they are part of a larger process of synthesis leaves the going back—or reductive—efforts of therapy quite hollow.

In China, as in Occidental number symbolism, one signifies the indivisible Whole, the *hen-to-pan*, the All-One. [62]

This *hen-to-pan* aspect, as Jung points out, is specific to every number. [65]

The Chinese idea of constructing two such rhythmically different Yang and Yin sequences is based on the assumption that the one-continuum in all its characteristics (such as polarity, centeredness, symmetry, dynamics, etc.), is constantly present in each number. . . . In other words, all numbers, according to the Chinese, are simply different qualitative configurations of the same one-continuum. [79]

As an example of Western number she refers to Plato:

Plato and many of the number theorists who followed him in antiquity considered all further numbers to arise by a *diairesis* (division) of the monad [the monad is the first existing "one"]. . . . Instead of assuming a division of the monad, I prefer to consider the latter running right through the whole number series. [63]

Both references confirm the presence in mathematical thinking that successive integers are different "amounts" of the number one. In the psychological equivalence of that statement, the symbols "two" and "three" and "four" are expressions of different phases of a single developmental process which starts and ends with one.

One can compare it [the one-continuum] to a "field" in which the individual numbers represent activated points. [63] (Figure 3, next page)

In the psychological translation of that statement, integers as symbols are indicators along the way of the process of facing and enduring conflict (two), synthesizing conflict (three) and reaching the condition of a cohesive and "non-split" mature personality (one again) which integrates the personality to a new breadth (four).

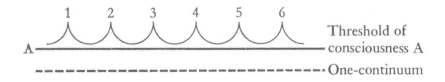

Figure 3. Activated points.

The Undifferentiated One

> According to this new hypothesis, for instance, the number two is not a halved or a doubled monad . . . but the symmetry aspect of the one-continuum. [64]

This simply restates her position thus far. But it sets the stage for a comment with, again, enormous consequences concerning the way Jung understood the analytic process and, in my opinion, concerning one of the most important qualities the analyst must bring to the consulting room.

> If this property of the number two is . . . confronted with the undifferentiated primal one, the number three arises out of this confrontation as their synthesis. . . . Strictly speaking this . . . step from two to three is a retrograde one, a reflection leading from two back to the primal one. [64]

> The latter [the primal one] is a mathematical symbol of the *unus mundus*. [66]

What does that mean, "confronted with the undifferentiated primal one"? How does the process we have described as one, two, three lead back to the primal one? How is the primal one the *unus mundus*?

The poet has provided the best answer to these questions. T.S. Eliot wrote in his *Four Quartets*:

> We shall not cease from exploration
> And the end of all our exploring
> Will be to arrive where we started
> And know the place for the first time.[50]

---

[50] "Four Quartets," p. 145. "Some things that happened for the first time | Seem to be happening again," from "Where Or When," by Rogers and Hart, says the same thing.

The origin and the goal are the same. But where the origin is unconscious, the goal is the conscious recognition and living of one's life. The *unus mundus*, meaning the inherited possibility for becoming what I can be, becomes real in time and space during the process of development. Bit by bit we make real what was inherent from the beginning.

To me it seems very clear that one of the main jobs of the analyst is to see and feel who that other essentially is. Beneath the chaos, the splits, the confusion, the contradictions, the "pathology," it is crucial for someone in the room—it won't be the analysand in the early stages of the work—to intuit in the heart the person "inside there" who is struggling to come into being. Originally the "primal unity" is a state of innocence, in the most negative sense. In that condition we are a mess of contradictions, a mush of inconsequential acts and denied emotions. We have a feeling of unity, simply because we don't experience our dis-unity. On the other hand that disunity is very precious because it holds the potential of our lives, albeit in seed form. Sooner or later, however, we will find ourselves in a situation where our feeling of paradisiacal completeness is shattered, like the dreamer in Jung's seminar. His contradictory behavior in the area of love was costing him his marriage, and he could see the effects of that breakdown on himself, his wife, and his children. Painfully he left paradise to look at his own conflict on the way to discovering his true Eros that was neither a wild orgy nor sentimental goop. As Jung wrote elsewhere,

> I always let [my patient] see that I was entirely on the side of . . . his future greater personality.[51]

Of course, before an analyst can put him- or herself on that side, he or she must feelingly see it in the other. No amount of technique or guidelines or norms will substitute. The psyche of the analysand must know there is a stereo process underway—a recognition of what *is,* seen in his or her current behavior on one hand, against the backdrop of what *was in potential from the beginning* and what *can be again in fact* on the other hand. Hence the reality of the person's suffering is confronted with a

---

[51] C.G. Jung, "Psychology and Religion," *Psychology and Religion,* CW 11, par. 80.

recognition, albeit tacit, in the analyst's soul of the primal unity of the other's potential and the end point of its realization. This, to my feeling, is, at least at first,[52] the primary job of the analyst.

The Axiom of Maria

Although it says nothing new, this aphorism holds such a place in Jung's work that it would nearly be a sin to omit mentioning the Axiom of Maria. Von Franz writes:

> The retrograde counting step leading from the number three to four [that is what I've just been talking about, how three leads to four and four is really one; four is like the new one] has been made historically famous by Maria Prophetissa's alchemical axiom: "Out of the One comes Two, out of Two comes Three, and from the Third comes the One as the Fourth." This means that the number three, taken as a unity related back to the primal one, becomes the fourth. This four is understood not so much to have "originated" progressively, but to have retrospectively existed from the very beginning. [64f.]

"Retrospectively existed from the very beginning" means returning to the place where we began and knowing it for the first time. Maria Prophetissa, also known as "Mary the Jewess," whether fact or legend, was an alchemist estimated to have lived anywhere between the first and third centuries A.D.

The Axiom of Maria is an oft-repeated phrase in the alchemical literature. The alchemists thought this business of one, two, three, four, and back to one was a changing characteristic of stuff inside matter as it went from worthless to gold. We, of course, understand the dictum metaphorically, and Jung was particularly fond of it.

Circumscribe

By this point in the chapter, the main objectives have been noted, with the bulk of the chapter conveying, from different angles, the paradox of multiplicity and unity. And so the rest of the chapter proceeds. Having

---

[52] Later the dialectic can be interiorized by the analysand.

observed the heart of her discussion, the remainder of the text continues along the same lines and is easily grasped. Here are some representative passages:

> All numbers are simply qualitatively differentiated manifestations of the primal one. [66]

> Every natural number becomes endowed with a quality of wholeness and meaning. [68]

> This wholeness adhering to each number was alive in primitive number concepts. We would benefit from reconsidering the primitive qualitative character of number, namely its wholeness aspect. [68f.]

> Number, taken qualitatively, is understood to function as a preconscious psychic principle of activity; each number must be thought of as containing a specific activity that streams forth like a field of force. From this standpoint numbers signify different rhythmic configurations of the one-continuum. [74f.]

Note the Buddhist example von Franz gives on page 80, again expressing the notion of the multiplicity containing a unity.

Chapter Summary

We have explored numbers as symbols of the Self's coming to consciousness. Knowing this capacity of symbolic expression that numbers possess is extremely helpful when they appear in dreams, and we can often readily observe how our suffering in life is part of a deeper process of integration. This is hopeful, though admittedly difficult to bear in mind during our psychic upheavals.

We have seen thus far in the book that numbers are a part of two domains, our inner continuum of potential and the outer material world. We have also explored the hypothesis that it is this similarity of structure between inner and outer that allows their essential unity to manifest in synchronistic moments. In this chapter we further probed into the nature of our inborn story, the Self, into how it first exists as an unconscious unity which is given, how it comes to conscious realization through a process of conflict and synthesis, a process portrayed very frequently in the form of numerical symbols. Each of the numerical phases of that *active* and *effective* process was touched on briefly. The next three chapters will continue to examine the "two," "three," and "four" phases of this route, which began from a unity and will end up there on a new level. The "one" thus finds different expressions along the way of its transformation until it enters into the daily life of a centered, solid, caring, generative, and continually maturing individual.

Chapter 5

The Number Two as the One-Continuum's Rhythm by Which Symmetries and Observables are Engendered

Symbolically, the number two represents the opposites. They can appear with a variety of meanings: as opposition or duality, as the threshold or transition to consciousness, as rhythm, as dual unity, and as a preparation for the future.

I am going to skip over a few points at the beginning of the chapter, so that we can keep our attention on the main theme of the Self's "numerically" coming to consciousness: Pauli's neutral language is discussed further in the Pauli-Jung letters.[53] The mathematical characteristics of two are common sense; to keep the discussion manageable I will limit the mathematical role of number to one reference in physics—that will at least give us a sense of the parallelism between the role of the number in physics and in the psyche without getting bogged down. The reference to complex numbers at the beginning of the chapter requires knowledge of higher mathematics that would drive a non-mathematician to despair.[54]

Duality

This is one of the dreams of our man with the arabesque.

> I am touring in my car near the Riviera. Someone tells me that the *route d'en haut et route d'en bas* [the high road and the low road][55] can be used from now on by those who stay for months in the country, that all cars have to go one way on the lower road, and the other way on the upper. These regulations change every day. Monday it is so, while on Tuesday it

---

[53] See *Atom and Archetype*, pp. 35, 40, 66f., 82, 105f., 111f., 117, 182f.

[54] For a layperson's mathematical description, see Herbert van Erkelens, "Wolfgang Pauli's Dialogue with the Spirit in Matter," pp. 48f.

[55] There are, in fact, two roads that run along parts of the coastline of southern France, one along the ocean, one along the ridge of the cliffs which, in their infinite charm, overlook sweeping vistas of the sun-drenched Mediterranean.

goes the other way, so that one could enjoy the beautiful view from every direction. . . . The visitors who were there for only a short time need not observe the regulations, and I thought it rather illogical that they could go just as they pleased.[56]

The back and forth is the two we saw in the arabesque drawing. The Riviera, along the southern coast of France on the Mediterranean, is one of the loveliest beaches in the world, where tasteful people romp about scantily clad. It is known as one of the erotic playgrounds of Europe. Remember what this man's problem is. The back and forth, the two, is his going back and forth, within himself, over several pairs of conflicting feelings, as introduced in the last chapter: "I can solve this, I can't solve this"; "I want to go to a prostitute, I don't want to go to a prostitute"; "I want my marriage to work, but I enjoy those fleshy prostitutes." The "two" is the image of doubting and self-argument that has started as he is beginning to face his problem. He is thrown from despair to hope, from lust to self-control, from loneliness to pleasure, and so on. It is a recognition of that tossing back and forth that starts when we honestly look at the primal unity in ourselves. When we have been going through life as a happy carrot, messing up our lives, but not seeing how, and then we face our emotional contradictions, that is when the "back and forth" duality theme appears. After we have bounced back and forth between the polarities with awareness and for a sufficient length of time, the third, the generating power of the psyche, is activated.

So the "visitors who were there for only a short time" would represent the attitude that does *not* want to commit to this process of facing conflict until it transforms. Dealing with conflict until it resolves creatively takes time, patience, and commitment, but the "tourist" attitude is the wish to shortcut the requirements. The "long-term" attitude suffers, tossed about by emotions—experienced as different, contradictory states of mind—until the third resolves the impasse. The "visitors" don't want to go through what is required so that the third can point the way; they want to dabble with emotional chaos and come up with some half-

---

[56] Jung, *Dream Analysis: Notes of the Seminar Given in 1928-30*, pp. 147ff.

hearted answer for themselves—usually, of course, to be paid for dearly later, often by their children. Psychological tourism neatly avoids facing any of that.

The Riviera dream is a classic two dream. Why is this understanding of psychological growth different from any other? Because, in my experience, what eventually emerges is a depth of selfhood that cannot be realized otherwise. There is something authentic, solid, and serene that comes to light over the course of time when we endure "two" on the way to "three." The solution is not "me-me-me"; it is a coherent and substantial individuality, grounded in depth. But it is the longer way.[57]

Real psychological work gets going in "two" dreams, just as counting gets going with "two." And it is no accident. There is no psychological work being done in "one" (as primary unity) dreams. There is psychological work being done in two dreams, just as there is the beginning of counting with the integer two. That is a simple example of the parallels in meaning being articulated by von Franz.

The Threshold of Matter

Recall we had the discussion and diagram in chapter 1, alluded to again in chapter 3, that when the electron changes energy states it gives off light. Well, the reverse is also true: light can become an electron. Light can turn into matter. Physicists can take the teensiest particle of light—light can be a particle as well as a wave, which is one of the "contradictions" of the Copenhagen Interpretation of Quantum Physics that says this is just the way the world is made—and these physicists can shoot the particle of light toward an atom. When they do that, the particle of light,

---

[57] This brings to mind the sanctuary of Demeter (the ancient Greek mother goddess) at Eleusis, outside Athens. Eleusis, modern Elefsina, is about a half-hour bus ride from downtown Athens. The remains of the sanctuary are open as a historical sight, and the area is, in the original sense of the word, awesome. After spending a day wandering around the archeological environs and then heading back to my hotel in Athens, I looked up at the modern buildings surrounding the sanctuary as I exited. I was moved by finding a restaurant just outside the gate by the name, written in English, of "Slow Food." I thought that said it all. The feminine way of creating consciousness by emergence is definitely slow food—but worth the patience.

called a "photon" of light, becomes an electron. So light can become an electron, and an electron is matter. But actually the situation is more complicated, because when light is converted into matter, it becomes *both* an electron and a *positron*, a negatively *and* a positively charged particle. In his very readable introduction to classical and quantum physics, physicist Robert March writes:

> The creation of an electron-positron pair [occurs] when a photon [of light] with sufficient energy passes close to an atomic nucleus. The nucleus must be present because the photon uses up part of its energy to create the mass of the positron and electron. The pair thus has less momentum than the original photon, and the excess momentum must be carried away by the nucleus.[58]

If all those scientific words make no sense, don't worry about it. The point for our purposes is that when a photon of light gets close to the nucleus of an atom, the light photon is changed into *two* particles with *mass*, that is to say that they become particles of *matter*. The creation of matter from light involves *two*. In physics, at the sub-atomic level, the creation of matter is tied to the number two.

So what? We will see, now, that the creation of consciousness, when it is expressed symbolically in dreams, is often likewise represented by the number two.[59] So two, in physics, as well as in dreams, is tied to the creation of the most basic stuff: matter in physics, consciousness in dreams. This is a prime example of the very significant resonance, so dear to von Franz, of similar numerical patterns in both physics and psychology, matter and psyche.

The Threshold of Consciousness

Thus, as two represents the threshold of matter in science, in psychology it represents the transition to consciousness along the journey to wholeness. In other words when we are about to become aware of something,

---

[58] Robert H. March, *Physics for Poets*, p. 240.

[59] The same is true for the role of two in myth. The enterprising reader can follow up this observation in von Franz's *Creation Myths*.

we are likely to dream of two of them. Two can mean conflict, and two can also mean coming to consciousness. Von Franz writes:

Identical duplications of objects in dreams, for instance, or in myths, point to the fact that a content *is just beginning to reach the threshold of consciousness* as a recognizable entity, taking the first step, as it were, toward manifestation. Jung says: [91f.]

Conscious perception means discrimination. Thus, structures arising from the unconscious will be distinguished when they reach the threshold of perception; such structures then appear to be doubled, but are two completely identical entities—the one and the other—since it has not yet become clear which is the one and which is the other.[60] [92]

And again she writes:

Whenever a latent unconscious content pushes up into consciousness, it appears first as a twofold oneness. [93]

We see this all the time in dreams: I am walking down the street, and there are two guys coming toward me, or two cats, or two dogs. When that theme appears in dreams it is a good bet that we are ready to deal with whatever those images symbolize. What was once the "unity" of unawareness, is now ready to become the "duality" of coming to the reality of consciousness. The above citation continues:

For this reason all cosmogonies begin their tales of the emergence of world-consciousness with a duality: creator twins, a god and his "helper," or, as in Genesis, the earth "without form and void," over which the Spirit of God moved. The traditional association of duality, on the one hand with matter, and on the other with the rise of consciousness, is not a matter of pure chance . . . appearing either as observable physical phenomena or as comparatively separable representations in our inner field of vision. [93f.]

Here is a typical dream of two in its meaning of coming to consciousness. It is from Edinger's peerless *Anatomy of the Psyche*:[61]

---

[60] Translated from C.G. Jung, *Seminar über Kinderträume*, 1938-39, p. 72. The passage can also be found in the English publication of the seminars: *Children's Dreams: Notes of the Seminar*, p. 140.

[61] Edward F. Edinger, *Anatomy of the Psyche*, p. 193.

It is night. There is the feeling that dawn is approaching. Two shepherds dressed in sheepskin, holding staffs and identical in looks are on a mountain path. There is an intense look in both their eyes that says they know they must go their separate ways. One has the look of the desire for vengeance and the other has a feeling of sadness. They embrace and kiss each other on the cheek with a kiss of peace and the one who had the feeling of sadness begins his climb up the mountain. The other shepherd pauses and looks at him as through to say, "I could have killed you!" and then turns and goes down the mountain and dawn has arrived.

Edinger reports that the dream comes from an individual at the end of a relationship based on mutual identity, a *participation mystique*—in pop psych language, a codependent relationship, one where people get along because they don't deal with the differences between them. Differences and disagreements are glossed over, but eventually resentment breaks out and paradise comes to an end. Such a friendship was coming to an end in the dreamer's life. The dream displays the content that the man projected onto his friend—the personal quality shared between him and his friend but which he saw only in his friend—and it is being seen in two parts: the two shepherds. As the man separates from that friend and withdraws the projection from him, the result is "two." He brings back the projection into himself, and when it shows up in the dream as being ready to come into consciousness, the dream portrays it not as one but as two. The birth of this awareness is then depicted as the dawning of light. That is the dream's way of speaking.[62]

---

[62] Compare the association of the number two with mythological depiction of the sun at the horizon. In ancient Egyptian art it is represented by a pair of lions, for instance. (Figure 4)

Figure 4. Scene from the Egyptian *Book of the Dead.*

Oscillation

Von Franz discusses time as rhythm on page 94. Two forms the basis of oscillation.

> Considered as a rhythm of movement, the number two represents a repetition, in the form of an oscillation. [94]

In the steamroller dream and the arabesque drawing, the fellow thought he was just going around in circles, but we saw that in the repeated back and forth oscillation over the same territory he was in fact moving toward the center.

In her discussion, von Franz links oscillation to time. Oscillation is simply a back and forth movement which, over time, starts to go somewhere. (Figure 5, next page) An oscillation pattern is the back and forth in its quality of moving forward toward synthesis. This is not really a new point, as when we discussed the back and forth we saw that it had the capacity to move into "three," the business of the next chapter. I mention her comments on the oscillatory meaning of two and its relation to time as background for the time aspect of number symbolism, those "special" moments of synchronicity, to be explored in chapter 13.

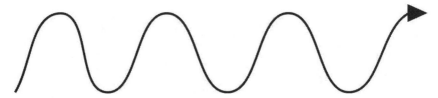

Figure 5. Swinging between extremes leads to forward movement.

Dual Unity

Another point that will be considered in more detail later, in chapters 10 and 11, the dual mandala, obviously makes use of the number two:

> More differentiated models of the *unus mundus* are double mandalas, and … they are especially liable to appear when the problem of time and synchronicity becomes constellated. [95]

This is an image that often sneaks into a dream in ways that are easily missed. Recently I saw a dream of a woman who had a considerable artistic gift and was seeking to find its expression in terms of who she really was. During this period of questioning she dreamed of starting her car with a key on a *two-ringed* key chain. That was a small detail in the dream but a very important one. Two mandalas were indicated. We will return to the dual mandala theme later.

The Future

It is clear by now that as soon as we discuss the number two, we are led to the number three, as duality seeks resolution in the third. Speaking of the back and forth von Franz writes:

> Its numerous repetitions then engender a "path," and thereby a time- or space-vector [in other words, a real psychological movement forward], the third element. [97]

Normally when we are in the "two" state of mind, the only place we think we are going is crazy. We can't make a decision. We have one feeling one moment, another feeling the next moment, as I have said. This can last for days, weeks or months, sometimes years—depending on the depth of the importance of the issue. It is very distressing. We don't feel in charge, and we aren't. We feel like a dog chasing its tail.

If we look at certain other psychologies, they will say this back and forth is the fragmentation of a psychological disorder. Jung, on the other hand, sees it as a typical step in the coming to consciousness of selfhood. For him the back and forth *is* the way to selfhood. Hence von Franz:

> This threeness is implicitly contained in the number two, but not yet explicitly indicated by its (two's) presence. [97]

The back and forth of the two, if maintained consciously, is a pregnancy for the emergence of the new direction in life. As one man, exasperated by being in the throws of this suffering, said to me, "You know, being born feels like dying."

All along, though we cannot experience it in the shuttlecock feeling of back and forth, the two opposites *are* slowly forming a new growth, a new start in life. I have returned to the back and forth theme again to stress that the back and forth is really a preparation for the future. In each to and fro, the opposites are nearing contact with each other until, so to speak, a conception occurs and a birth is prepared. This is certainly hard to imagine when we feel so torn apart, but it is so.

A remarkable example of the two giving rise to the future, the third of the next chapter, is to be found in Jung's life, during his 1944 heart attack. While he was hovering near death he had this vision:

> I . . . was . . . in the Pardes Rimmonim, the garden of pomegranates, and the wedding of Tifereth with Malchuth was taking place. . . . It was the mystic marriage as it appears in the Cabbalistic tradition. I cannot tell you how wonderful it was. . . . Gradually the garden of pomegranates faded away and changed. There followed the Marriage of the Lamb, in a Jerusalem festively bedecked. I cannot describe what it was like in detail. These were ineffable states of joy.[63]

Pardes Rimmonim is a Cabbalistic tract from the sixteenth century. Cabbalism is the mystical tradition within Judaism, with roots partly in me-

---

[63] *Memories, Dreams, Reflections*, p. 294 and note.

dieval Europe. In Cabbalistic doctrine, Malchuth and Tifereth are two of the ten spheres of divine manifestation in which God emerges from his hidden state. They represent the female and male principles within the Godhead.

Though in Jung's vision we have a remarkable example of the two in their creative aspect, we don't see the third. But the third is evidenced in Jung's starting his major authorship at this point in his life. All the works I mentioned in the introduction followed after Jung's heart attack and this dream. *They* are the third.

Imagery of the sort in Jung's vision means we are looking for, or are preparing ourselves for, a significant development in our psychological, emotional behavior, and in our creative substance. When we read early Jung, I mean before 1944, and compare the depth of his writing to the late Jung, after 1944, there is a world of difference. Jung's final writings are undiluted essence. They are cherished vintage Bordeaux.[64]

---

[64] For a handsome appreciation and elucidation of Jung's work as rare wines, see Daryl Sharp's series (four books), *Jung Uncorked: Rare Vintages from the Cellar of Analytical Psychology.*

Chapter 6

The Number Three as a Rhythmic Configuration of Progressive Actualizations in Human Consciousness and the Material Realm

The number three, symbolically speaking, depicts an understanding of psychological growth unique to Jungian psychology. It's Jung's observation that the "third thing" which resolves endured conflict is not consciously created: it is formed outside the power of the ego. The resolution is a creative act that is given to us, and the emphases are on creative and given. Call it grace if you want. The resolution to the most important conflicts in life is not something we could ever have thought up. It is how truly new things come into the world. They are generated from within—oops, and from without. We don't make them happen but we do make it *possible* for them to happen through our consciously carrying the duality of conflict—facing it, not pretending it doesn't exist, resisting the temptation to identify with one side only. And in that suffering for, and appearance of, the third we again find our true individuality, our true gifts, our true strength to make them real. The inborn possibility of our lives, a piece of our real story, is thus brought to life. We become less fragmented: the unity within, and encompassing, what had previously tried to tear us apart enters conscious living. We find our strength, but it is strength always at the same time ultimately mixed with the softness of receptivity and the accustomed longing of waiting.

Jung's Life and Work

It will be worthwhile to take a moment to recognize in what way this perception of growth and healing fit into Jung's life. Jung had the insight in his night sea journey, from 1913 to 1928, his period of personal confusion and searching after he split from Freud. What he observed in himself first, and then in his analysands who were working at depth, is how the third thing is created from inside ourselves when we consciously en-

73

dure conflict. He wondered if he was seeing a process that was active merely in himself or maybe it was a cultural artifact just specific to Europeans—or was it something that was part of a cross-cultural psychological inheritance? Then in 1928 he received a copy of "The Secret of the Golden Flower" from Richard Wilhelm in China. "The Secret of the Golden Flower" is a Taoist text,[65] thought to have originated in the eighth century CE.[66] It describes the process of meditation and enlightenment according to the Taoist understanding. Jung took this as a hint that in his psychological journey he had recognized something prodigious.

The text impressed Jung because it illustrated the Taoist conception of enlightenment in exactly the same way that he had already conceived the nature of psychological transformation originating from our core. He then found in medieval alchemy an analogous and meaningful depiction of the selfsame process whereby the duality of conflict resolves into the production of a third. One of the texts that illustrates this clearly is a series of woodcuts in a tractate called *Rosarium Philosophorum* from 1550. In their medieval symbolic language the pictures express what the alchemists thought was literally going on in the material they were cooking while Jung explored its metaphorical significance.

I have selected a sampling of those images so that we can have at least a beginning sense of their meaning.[67] (See next few pages.) Jung pointed out the pictures' depiction of: a first unity represented by the fountain (Fig. 6-1), morphing into a king and queen with the sun and the moon in the fountain picture becoming associated with the king and queen here (Fig. 6-2), who unite (Fig. 6-3), die and produce a third thing depicted as the little ascending man (Fig. 6-4); the little man then descends (Fig. 6-5), and when he does the pair turn into a unity (Fig. 6-6).

---

[65] Taoism is an ancient Chinese religion; its thought generally focuses on nature and the men-cosmos correspondence. Tao is generally translated as "path" or "way."

[66] "The Secret of the Golden Flower," New World Encyclopedia.

[67] The original 1550 tractate contains 20 images of which Jung interpreted 10. See "The Psychology of the Transference," in *The Practice of Psychotherapy,* CW 16.

ROSARIVM

Wyr sindt der metall anfang vnd erste natur /
Die kunst macht durch vns die höchste tinctur.
Reyn brunn noch wasser ist meyn gleych/
Ich mach gesund arm vnd reych.
Vnd bin doch jtzund gyftig vnd dötlich.

Succus

Figure 1

Figure 6-1.

PHILOSOPHORVM.

Nota bene: In arte noſtri magiſterij nihil eſt ſecretum
celatū à Philoſophis excepto ſecreto artis, quod artis
non licet cuiquam reuelare, quod ſi fieret ille ma
lediceretur , & indignationem domini incur=
reret , & apoplexia moreretur. ⸹ Quare om=
nis error in arte exiſtit , ex eo, quod debitam

C ij

Figure 2

Figure 6-2.

CONIVNCTIO SIVE
Cortus.

O Luna durch meyn vmbgeben/vnd susse mynne/
Wirstu schön/ starck/vnd gewaltig als ich byn.

O Sol/ du bist vber alle liecht zu erkennen/
So bedarsstu doch mein als der han der hennen.

ARISLEVS IN VISIONE.

Coniunge ergo filium tuum Gabricum dile-
ctiorem tibi in omnibus filijs tuis cum sua sorore
Beya

Figure 5

Figure 6-3.

Figure 7

Figure 6-4.

PHILOSOPHORVM

ANIMÆ IVBILATIO SEV
Ortus seu Sublimatio.

ⅾie ſchwingt ſich die ſele hernidder/
Vnd erquickt den gereinigten leychnam wider-

L iij

Figure 9

Figure 6-5.

PHILOSOPHORVM.

hie ift geboren die eddele Aeyferin reich/
Die meifter nennen fie jhrer dochter gleich.
Die vermeret fich/gebiert kinder ohn zal/
Sein vnd&lich rein/vnnd ohn alles mahl.

Die

Figure 10

Figure 6-6.

The Taoist pictures[68] resonated very closely with those drawings in terms of a unitary figure in the belly of the meditating man (Stage 2) eventually becoming a multiplicity (Stage 4). (Figures 7-1 to 7-4) The woodcut images subsequent to that depiction have been lost, but the text goes on to describe the multiplicity coming together again in the production of a golden flower, hence the text's name; and when the multiplicity reunites into the unity of the golden flower, the mediating person has achieved enlightenment.[69] Once more there is the synthesis of a new product out of a union of previously disparate parts.

Meditation. Stage 1: Gathering the light.

Figure 7-1.

[68] Richard Wilhelm and C.G. Jung, *The Secret of the Golden Flower.*
[69] Ibid., pp. 33, 49, 54f., 61, 65.

圖形現兒嬰

他日雲飛方見真人朝上帝

一潛身真到紫微宮
一朝踁出球光外
變現神通不可窮
潛龍今已化飛龍
長養空虛
內外無虛
沈潛永休
神水冷凍

他云是你主人翁
念玆在玆
我聞空中誰氏子
轆轆若存
歲過孫孫孫包空
趯趯守離
氣穴法名無盡藏
行住坐卧

此時丹熟更須慈母惜嬰兒

夫嫌暗一真
孕娘始之于
傳此指變來
精混其氣樹
其神固細火
小供禮其真

Meditation, Stage 2: Origin of a new being in the place of power.

Figure 7-2.

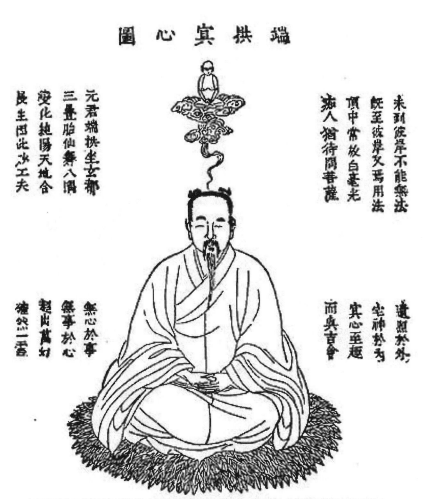

端拱冥心圖

元君端拱坐玄都
三疊胎仙舞八隅
變化絕陽天地合
長生因此水工夫

長生因此水工夫

未到彼岸不能無法
既至彼岸又焉用法
頂中常放白毫光
痴人猶待問菩薩

無心於事
無事於心
超出萬幻
確然一香

遺照於外
宅神於為
寂心至趣
而與吉會

Meditation, Stage 3: Separation of the spirit-body for independent existence.

Figure 7-3.

Meditation, Stage 4: The centre in the midst of the conditions.

Figure 7-4.

With the observation of this parallel between Western alchemical symbolism and East Asian Taoism, Jung felt confident in saying that the process of conflict and synthesis in a third that he had observed during the emotional passage from loss of certainty to the birth of individuality was an inborn one.

A Dream Example

I would like to discuss two dreams that depict the shift from two to three. Both were dreamed in the same night by a man in the second half of life. The man was proud of his very considerable success, though he began life in a family of quite modest circumstances.[70]

> In the first dream he sees two alternating substances. He is confused because he can't get them both in view at the same time. As the dream progresses he finally is able to see them side-by-side. And, in fact, he wakes up from the dream. He goes back to sleep and has another dream. In the second dream he is with a friend of his, but gets bored and leaves. He next goes looking for a plane connection he is supposed to make on Delta airlines. But he has a rental car which he has to take back before he can get on the Delta flight. In the frustration of trying to return the car he wakes up.

His association to the friend was as follows: he is a man of very meager upbringing, a working-class kid who became a successful well-to-do doctor. A lot of his problems in life stem from his being torn between his working-class roots and the attention he gets for being a wealthy, successful doctor.

Let's interpret the dreams. The duality expressed in the second dream lies in the friend's being both a working-class fellow and a successful doctor. So the friend in the dream would represent the dreamer's own conflict between his working-class upbringing and his successful, professional accomplishments. That is most likely the polarity that is shown at the beginning of the first dream where he is trying to get both substances in view, that is, to comprehend that he has the two sides to his personal-

---

[70] As did I.

ity—the humble beginnings and the success which likes to dazzle. In the dreamer's life at the time of the dream, the two sides were in fact working against him. Whereas some people might find an easy transition from the realization of their humble roots to an appreciation of their worldly success, the dreamer had not.

Just as an aside, there are interesting similarities here to Jung's story. He came from very humble origins and then obviously achieved significant worldly success. Somehow, from my years in Zürich, I have a cassette tape of Jung speaking in a seminar, so it sounds, to a group of young psychiatrists. I don't remember exactly how I received it, and as far as I know it hasn't been published. In any case, Jung is speaking in his Basel German dialect. I have a Swiss friend who is from Basel, and I told her about this tape. She excitedly replied that she would very much like to hear it. I said, "Okay, but what is the excitement about?" She said, "I want to hear what Basel German he is speaking, because he was raised in an area of Basel that spoke a very working-class version of the language. I want to hear whether in this professional and public setting he is speaking his working-class Basel German or whether he is speaking the more 'refined' Basel German." It turns out Jung was speaking his working-class Basel German. That is to say: for him there was no conflict between his origins and his success. He didn't need to put on airs. He had the ability to own that he came from humble roots and to be proud of it and, still, to mix that in with his professional success.

As I said, at the time of the dream, the dreamer was not able to do this. He hid his roots in his success. Therefore the achievement was a bit empty. He was, for a time, a lonely man because half of him simply was not there in his new, successful, identity. And he could become fascinated with the rich and famous to his detriment.

So the first dream presents the man's conflict in the two substances, which is to say he is becoming aware of them. The dream starts off with "two."

Delta airlines in the second dream, then, would be the three. We see conflict in the "two" images, and then we see him in search of resolution. In a subtle way, like in the name of an airline, number symbolism sneaks in to the dream. So Delta airlines, the triangle, the three, would be the resolution of the split between humble and rich. It would be the solution generated by the unconscious. But note that before the man can get to the three, the Delta, he has to return his rental car. The rental car would likely stand for his borrowed identity, the temptation to a borrowed big-shot identity. That is what he has to give up before the unconscious can become creative and before it can show him the resolution of his conflict in the "three" image.

Release

> But every tension of opposites culminates in a release, out of which comes the "third." In the third, the tension is resolved and the lost unity is re-stored. Unity, the absolute One, cannot be numbered, it is indefinable and unknowable; only when it appears as a unit, the number one, is it know-able, for the "Other" which is required for this act of knowing is lacking in the condition of the One. Three is an unfolding of the One to a condition where it can be known—unity become recognizable.[71] [102]

How does unity become real and recognizable? Only by our going through that period where the two sides of ourselves that were in con-flict, which we didn't see when we were blissfully unaware, become evi-dent to us *as* a conflict, and we stay aware of them both until they are resolved. Jung writes:

> Had it [the initially unconscious conflict] not been resolved into the polar-ity of the One and the Other, it would have remained fixed in a condition devoid of every quality.[72] [102]

Von Franz sums up:

> Accordingly, the number three stands behind dynamic actualizations of the one-continuum in time-space dimensions and in our consciousness. [102]

In other words, the one-continuum is our potential future identity in its

---

[71] C.G. Jung, "A Psychological Approach to the Dogma of the Trinity," *Psychology and Religion*, CW 11, par. 180.
[72] Ibid.

unknown state. That identity becomes manifest through conflict. When the conflict is resolved, knowledge of the real self comes into being: it has gone through a process of differentiation and recognition. Otherwise we are just an unspecified blob of conflicting tendencies. The stabilizing movement from two to three is like a magical movement. What the ego has to do is to take responsibility for the "two," the back and forth. Then the unconscious gets busy to generate images of the "three"—the birth of true coherence, substance, and individuality.

Direction in Time

> Taken as rhythm or dynamism, three thus introduces a *directional* element into the oscillatory rhythm of two ... . [103, emphasis added]

At first we were the ping-pong ball between two sets of emotions. As established, what eventually emerges is that we have actually been going somewhere, moving forward in life.[73] Previously there was only a feeling of being swamped by conflicting pulls. But with three a forward movement or a development of life can be seen out of the back and forth. The continuing quote expands that idea:

> ... whereby spatial and temporal parameters can be formed. . . . In terms of content the number three therefore serves as the symbol of a dynamic process. [104]

What are "spatial and temporal parameters"?

At this point in the process of the Self's coming to consciousness, "things" in reality, in space and time, begin to change. It is at this point that synchronicities take on a particular importance. In these periods of development I tell people to pay very close attention to what crosses their path *now*. Before, when they were in the two phase, they were absorbed in their own confusion and misery. But when the three phase comes along the world will react. Another way to say that, which we have

---

[73] Jung describes an engaging example of this in his essay "A Study in the Process of Individuation," *The Archetypes and the Collective Unconscious*, CW 9i, pars. 525ff. Observe in particular the development within pictures 6, 7, and 8, discussed from par. 569 through par. 595.

touched on and will pursue further, is that the quality of time changes. Previously we were in a phase where we had to withdraw from the world, simply because we were inwardly consumed. Now we are in a phase where we have to meet the world. But not only that, and this is the big deal: *the world comes to meet us.* So we have to pay attention to the outer world in the three phase. Because if we don't, we could let opportunities go by much to our loss, where in the two phase it wouldn't have mattered. If we let certain opportunities go by in the three phase, we miss very important chances for our development. As von Franz mentions in footnote 5 on page 103, the number three has been linked to the *vinculum amoris*, the love bond—which is to say in the number three phase we find our way back to the world with love, Eros. That is where and how the newly conscious Self wants to live.

The Matter of Fate

Remember the title of the book links the words number *and* time. When this three phenomenon is active, the quality of time has changed. This, suitably, leads us to a consideration of fate. In qualitatively different moments of time, opportunities, both inside and in the outer world, are presented. These must be seized, or the point of all the conflict and intended development is lost. We have to be astute and notice when the world is coming to meet us in order for us to put the new development we are in the process of achieving into the real world. In my own life, for example, when I was working on *At the Heart of Matter*, I was wondering if I hadn't been wasting my time (and life) probing into the inner world of Wolfgang Pauli, a central figure in the narrative. From certain dreams, it did seem that the inquiry gave room for and brought into synthesis (the "three") the diverse parts of my history—science, psychology, religion, the East (I had lived there in the Peace Corps)—but still I wondered. Then I dreamed that I would be getting the material I would be working on for the rest of my life. That is all the dream said. The next day in the mail I received a package from esteemed friend and colleague David Lindorff[74] containing copies of the Pauli-von Franz correspon-

---

[74] Lindorff, *Pauli and Jung: The Meeting of Two Great Minds.*

dence he had found while scouring archives in Switzerland. Dave is reaching the end of his full life and wanted to pass this material on for safekeeping and future possible research. I had no inkling he—very generously—would be doing this.

Psychological growth is dependent on both a resolved inner world and the right opportunity in the outer world.[75] We need opportunities, we need the *right* opportunities, we need a chance for the right relationship, we need a chance for the right job, if we are in the job we need the right connections—or what good is all the talent? If we are living the life that is generated by the Self, just as the Self generates those new possibilities, it also "generates" the place in the world that can use those abilities, attitudes, and insights we have developed. Otherwise we stagnate with developed potential that cannot find its way to actualization. It is important to respond to the outer opportunities that appear at the right time and that can receive our inner accomplishments.

The reverberation between inner and outer, at definite, fated moments of time, is expressed in mythology. Von Franz writes that

> in the mythological productions of the unconscious psyche, underworld divinities are particularly likely to appear in triadic form. . . . According to Jung, they [the triadic underworld divinities] represent the flow of psychic energy, indicating a connection with time and fate.[76] [104]

Subterranean Hecate (Figure 8) for example, protects crossroads, the place where decisions are made and roads are taken. Passing Cerberus (Figure 9) on the way to the underworld, the hero is shown the next step in his fated journey while in the realm below.[77] Three is about the hand of fate and its role in redemption.

---

[75] Jung, *Dream Analysis*: "That is often so in analysis, external circumstances make it impossible to go ahead," (p. 147) and "One always is making the mistake of not counting on miracles." (p. 559)

[76] *Seminar über Kinderträume*, 1938-39, p.144. The passage can also be found in the English publication of the seminars: *Children's Dreams: Notes of the Seminar*, p. 204.

[77] In Book VI of the *Aeneid*, after passing Cerberus on his way to the underworld, Aeneas is shown future generations of Rome. Immediately prior to his descent, "The Sibyl cried out: 'Now is the time to ask your destinies.'" (Virgil, *The Aeneid*, Book VI, lines 71-73, p. 161.)

Figure 8. *Hecate,* by William Blake.

Two Additional Points

The chapter ends with von Franz's commentary on two items. One is the connection between the I Ching and DNA, that is, three as a link between the psyche and matter. The other is a dream of Wolfgang Pauli's. I have reviewed both of these elsewhere,[78] so I will make just barest mention of them here.

---

[78] *At the Heart of Matter*, pp. 127ff. (the I Ching and DNA), 151ff. (the dream).

Figure 9. *Cerberus,* by William Blake.

The I Ching's oracular pattern is created by a throw of three coins six times. From the numerical results of these throws, patterns are generated. By consulting the book's commentary on the patterns, we can find a response to our question at the particular moment of time the query is put. So three is the basis of this read on the meaning of our psychic situation, that is, the larger picture of life as daily details may express it. Likewise RNA, which is transcribed from DNA, is made up of codons of three molecules. The foundation of our physiological fate is made up of the same three-pattern as the building blocks for the patterns of the I Ching—which communicates the meaning of a situation in life with respect to our psychological fate. Again there is a numerical correspondence between psychic and physical reality. According to von Franz, this correspondence forms the backdrop of the unity between psyche and matter.

On page 108 von Franz presents a dream of Wolfgang Pauli's.[79] The night before the dream he drew a Star of David on a piece of paper and wrote out certain themes of his personality at its apices, in order to see a pattern in his life. Then he dreamed:

A Chinese woman (elevated to the rank of a "Sophia") is present with two men. I am the fourth. She says to me: "You must allow us to play every conceivable combination of chess." In a subsequent half-waking fantasy she announced to the dreamer, in a numinous voice: "In your drawings one element is perfectly correct and other transitory and false. It is correct that the lines number six, but it is false to draw six points. See here—" and I saw:

Figure 10. Sketches from Pauli's dream.

—a square with clearly marked off diagonals [Figure 10]. "Can you see now finally the four and the six? Four spatial points and six lines or six pairs out of four points. They are the same six lines that exist in the I Ching. There the six, containing three as a latent factor, are correct. Now observe the square more closely: four of the lines are of equal length, the other two are longer—they are "irrationally related." There is *no* such figure with four points and six equal lines. *For this reason symmetry cannot be statically produced and a dance results.* The *coniunctio* refers to the exchange of places during this dance. One can also speak of a game or rhythms and rotations. *Therefore the three, already contained in a latent form in the square, must be dynamically expressed.*

Take a look at an octahedron (double pyramid, Figure 11). If you can imagine looking down on this shape from the top, you will see the boxed diagonal cross hairs of the second shape in Pauli's dream depicted by figure 10. The implication of the dream-woman's statement is that he is looking at an octahedron from above. Now, the octahedron is the model

---

[79] Herbert van Erkelens, "Wolfgang Pauli and the Chinese *Anima* Figure," pp. 38ff.

of the Self that Jung develops in his book *Aion*.[80] He uses that shape as a metaphor for the coming to consciousness of selfhood. The point at the bottom of the octahedron would represent the unconscious unity, which is then differentiated into its four components, and that is then synthesized into the new whole, the top point of the figure.

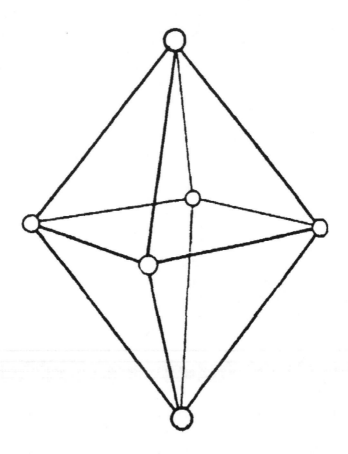

Figure 11. Octahedron.

---

[80] CW 9ii, chapter 14.

Don't become confused by my saying that the first unconscious state is differentiated into four components where earlier I said that the unity is broken up into a duality. The important point is that the unconscious unity is broken up into its constituent—often conflicting—parts. And since we have acknowledged that the dreams use numbers qualitatively, what they are driving at, whether the parts are numbered as two or four or whatever, is that the first unity is eventually seen in its various parts which were not felt as problematic before the process of inner scrutiny such as occurs in analytic work. So this image of the octahedron, indicating unconscious unity developing into conflict and later synthesized into a conscious whole, is a three-step process (unity, duality/multiplicity, resolution). That is the reference in the dream to *"the three, already contained in a latent form in the square."* The three is the dynamism of development inherent in our conflicting pieces, but it is not activated (i.e., is latent) until we begin investigating what and who those pieces in us are.

Von Franz comments on the dream:

> For now it is important to note the emphasis on the number three, or six, as the figure of a dynamic process enabling the totality symbol to manifest itself, in all its latent possibilities, in a temporal succession so that it does not congeal into a static symmetry or harmony. [109]

The totality seeks to "manifest itself," meaning the unconscious state actually "wants" to go to a conscious state through a temporal sequence and does not "want" to stay stuck in a previous level of unawareness. As life proceeds into its second half, it is the words "congeal" and "static" which become so important. The understanding of growth and development that Jung has put forward shows very clearly there is every reason to believe that the enriching of life can continue through to the very end. "Congealed" and "static" do not have to be the inevitable conclusions to life.

Chapter 7

The Number Four as the One-Continuum's Model of Wholeness in All Relatively Closed Structures of Human Consciousness and in the Body

Three is the big Jungian number. Four is the bigger Jungian number. Basically, four is representative of completeness and the relativization of consciousness. What is meant by that? With three we are dealing with an image of something new being generated from within ourselves. The danger is that we become rigid with it. We stick to it apart from anything else. We are fascinated by the new thing and try to explain everything by it. Four is that stage when the three enters into reality and collides with what is; it is accordingly reshaped, modified, humanized, relativized. In three we are attached in a dogmatic fashion to the new realization. In four we distinguish between *the* truth and *our* truth. Three proselytizes. Four accepts.

Parts of this chapter are very technical. If we are reading the book for the first time, I don't believe we will be remiss in skipping them, concentrating, instead, on the main themes of the chapter.

Dream Examples

The following are Wolfgang Pauli's dreams that Jung published in *Psychology and Alchemy*.[81] Jung describes the dreams:

> In a primeval forest. An elephant looms up menacingly. Then a large ape-man . . . threatens to attack the dreamer with a club. . . . ["The dreamer is terrified."][82]

The issue is this attacking ape-man. These dreams occurred after Pauli's first marriage had fallen apart and his mother had committed suicide when Pauli's father abandoned her. All of this happened within a very

---

[81] "Individual Dream Symbolism in Relation to Alchemy," *Psychology and Alchemy*, CW 12, pars. 44ff.
[82] Ibid., par. 117.

short time during his first years in Switzerland. Pauli fell apart, started drinking and getting into brawls. The outburst of unruly behavior would be symbolized by the ape-man. How could Pauli come to grips with that? The following "four" dream addresses the question.

> Many people are present. They are all walking to the left around a square. The dreamer is not in the center but to one side. They say that a gibbon [a kind of ape] is to be reconstructed.[83]

The gibbon's reconstruction would represent Pauli's ability to transform and humanize the previous ape-man. The dangerous ape-man is an image of Pauli's instincts run amuck because he allowed so little of healthy instinct into his daily life. His instincts were like a caged animal that sought to escape its prison in bursts of wild behavior. At this point in his life Pauli was identified with his role of "famous professor," and that left little room for his down-to-earth nature. To reconstruct the gibbon would mean to develop a much more natural personality, less socially affected, less oriented toward status, for example. Jung writes:

> A leftward movement is equivalent to a movement in the direction of the unconscious. ... Now he [the gibbon] is to be "reconstructed," and this can only mean that the anthropoid—man as an archaic fact—is to be put together again.[84]

"Man as an archaic fact" means the real, first, true personality. This is another way of expressing what we have described before in terms of the transcendental continuum, the inborn story, who we were meant to be from birth, and so on. "Archaic" is used in the sense of our identity being there when we came into the world.[85] Why "put together again"? Because, strangely, the potential for selfhood often lies in all our ignored instinct. The neglected, genuine identity is, by definition, the undeveloped part of ourselves, often lost in the parts of life that we have ignored. What was ignored in Pauli's case was his natural humanity—that had

---

[83] Ibid., par. 164.

[84] Ibid,, pars. 166, 169.

[85] Thus later in this essay Jung speaks of "an order in the unconscious," "a pre-existent ground plan." Ibid., par. 189.

been overlaid by all the requirements of his success which pressed on him to be a fancy high-brow fellow. Within his "wildness" was the real Pauli, the person not defined by public and professional opinion. The challenge of the dream is to feel the more natural and genuine personality within the wild behavior, without having to go to the extremes of destructiveness, and to allow the creation of new and more realistic attitudes as the dreams bring back, piece by piece, images of Pauli's real self. The dreamer is circumambulating, trying to discover who he is from within the instinctual chaos. He is finding a piece of himself here, a piece of himself there—as the dreams weave him into a new person.

Jung continues:

> [The dreamer] "not in the center but to one side" is a striking indication of what will happen to his ego: *it will no longer be able to claim the central place* . . .

This is the relativization that we see in four—

> . . . but must presumably be satisfied with the position of a satellite, or at least of a planet revolving around the sun. Clearly the important place in the center is reserved for the gibbon about to be reconstructed.[86]

The dreamer is off center and the gibbon is to be reconstructed in that center. So the real Self will populate the center. The ego is only peripheral to it. This is the shift to four.

There are two important points here in light of our discussion of "four." One is the pre-existent ground plan trying to come into consciousness as Pauli transforms his behavior. The other is the relativization of the ego. It is no longer dominant. The ego is no longer identified with the inner center, no longer self-righteously at the center of everything, nor is it identified with its "rightness" in human relationships. Four indicates the realized birth of a fresh part of legitimate selfhood which, at the same time, is open to other influences from without as much as it has been and is open to influences from within.

The birth of selfhood and a recognition of the relative importance of

---

[86] Ibid., par. 175 [italics added].

the ego vis-à-vis the Self always go hand-in-hand. Real people are accessible. They are emotionally available. It is the false idea of individuality of our age which thinks "unique" means "above." If your car is different and your house is different, you are unique. No. Selfhood and humanity are indistinguishable.

Mathematical Characteristics

From the beginning of the chapter until page 122 von Franz summarizes the mathematical characteristics of the number four. The discussion is detailed. I will mention just a few of her points.

One example [114]: four is the number of wholeness and, geometrically speaking, it takes four points to form a solid body. With one there is a point. With two points there is a line. With three points there is a plane (a flat surface). With four points there is a solid body. It takes four points to define a solid body. (Figure 12)

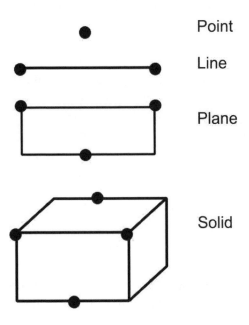

Figure 12. Point, line, plane, solid body.

Another example:

> The fact that mankind's repeated attempts to establish an orientation to-
> ward wholeness possess a quaternary appears to correspond to an arche-
> typal psychic structural predisposition in man. [115]

For example, compasses have four points. And when Native Americans
lay out a sand painting they do so by way of four points. She sees the
parallel between practices of outer, objective orientation and the subjective orientation of inner quaternary symbols.

The next example, to me, is definitive:

> Minkowski's and Einstein's *four*-dimensional model of the universe
> makes its appearance in present-day theoretical physics. [115, emphasis
> added]

The number four plays the key role in Einstein's new physics where the
number three plays the key role in Newton's physics. To locate an object
in space in Newtonian physics I need to tell three things: how far something is to the right or left of me, how far it is above or below me, and
how far it is in front of or in back of me. So it takes three dimensions to
define a spot in space in the old, classical physics.

But with Einstein this changes. He says that Newton's system is okay
if the other point I am dealing with is at rest. But if the point is zooming
by me at, say, half the speed of light, or if I am zooming by it at, say, half
the speed of light, the length of what is space actually contracts the faster
it or I go. Any given measure of length varies from one point of reference to the other as the speed between those two points is very fast. The
length of space shortens to zero as we approach the speed of light. The
faster we go, the shorter things get. So to locate something in a point in
space, if I am traveling very fast, I can't just report the distances, because
these distances are different in my frame of reference from what they are
in another, say a stationary object's, frame of reference. I know that
doesn't sound right to the common sense understanding of space, but
Einstein's relativity theories have overturned all those common under-
standings of space and distance. So I have to report how fast I am moving, if my speed is anywhere near the speed of light, so we know how far

"far" is. To locate a point in space we have to know three points of distance and the speed of movement between the measurer and the measured. Four measurements are necessary to locate a point in space when there is rapid (close to the speed of light) movement involved. Well, at least at the moment, people are not able to travel anywhere near the speed of light, but subatomic particles do and the light streaming in from other galaxies does too; so in certain situations Einstein's relativity of space (and time) makes all the difference.[87]

Von Franz draws a parallel between Jung's saying the image of wholeness is based on four and modern science's saying four determinants are needed to locate a point in space. That is to say, the foundation of the psyche is fourfold as the foundation of space-time is fourfold.[88] The parallelism between the structure of the psyche and the structure of the material world is impressive.

Three and Four

Consider the following passage in *Number and Time:*

> The difficult step from three to four would, according to this hypothesis, also be the progression from the infinitely conceivable to finite reality. [122]

"Infinitely conceivable" would be the transcendental continuum; it would be the genuine possibility, the given pattern of our life. "Finite reality" means to put the possibility into daily events, to actualize our potential.

The incommensurability of three dimensions to the fourth ... [is] based on

---

[87] This is a simple and simplistic description. For the brave of heart I have included a slightly more detailed account of Einstein's theory in the appendix. Einstein's work is important in light of the current discussion because it shows a fundamental shift in our understanding of matter, space, and time, while Jung's work shows an equally basic shift in our understanding of psyche, spirit, and meaning.

[88] Is it an accident that within twenty-two years Nietzsche said the Trinitarian God is dead *(Thus Spake Zarathustra,* 1883, p. 6), and Einstein said trintarian space is no longer valid (1905)? The breakdown of three for four is the theme of our age. Jung was part of this.

the inclusion (no longer avoidable) of the observer in his *wholeness* within the framework of his process of understanding. [122]

There is no longer an articulated "truth." There is: "Here's my truth." Think of fundamentalists. We can never say to them, "This is my point of view, and that is your point of view." It will be pointed out that we are wrong and they are right. That is the three state of mind at its worst. With "three" there is an objective judgment that is being made—so says the judge.

These processes are based on individual experience occurring in a particular and distinctive way. [122]

That means that what we say is our point of view.

But their results are not unalloyed subjectivity, insofar as the realizations taking place are fashioned not only out of the subject's ego but out of his "objective" psychic wholeness, which participates in the surroundings and in the actual moment of time. [122]

Von Franz is not in accord with a typically contemporary conviction which says "everything is subjective." That is akin to the postmodern point of view: "knowing is merely subjective."[89] For her there is such a thing as objectivity. She is, however, a little bit in sympathy with the current "everything is subjective" position in this sense: the objectivity that is within us can never be known fully objectively; it can only be known with due regard to subjectivity. Points of view may be subjective though inner facts can be objective. Don't throw up your hands!! This sounds like philosophical hair-splitting, but it has important psychological consequences. Let me explain.

I have come across marriage counselors who tend to treat what each person says in the therapy as "a point of view." "Oh, you see it this way" to one's spouse, and "Oh, you see it that way," to the other spouse. They don't acknowledge there is some objective thing going on between the

---

[89] In postmodernism there is an "emphasis on skepticism, especially concerning objective reality." Likewise postmodern deconstruction "is meant to undermine the frame of reference and assumptions that underpin the text or the artifact." ("Postmodernism," Wikipedia)

people. There *is* an objective interaction happening between them, though, it is true, it is normally perceived through each subject.

I remember a couple in marriage counseling. I was consulting with the wife, and the couple was seeing a family therapist. Every time this poor woman complained about her awful husband, the marriage therapist would say, "that is your point of view, your response is conditioned by such-and-such an event in the past, etc." Then one day at home the husband punched his wife in the face. She was seriously bruised and for a time disfigured. I wanted to ask the therapist whose point of view that was. In many arguments it *is* helpful to say, "Here is how I see it," and so on. But at a certain point it is foolish to treat everything going on in the relationship as "subjective." The punch in the face was not subjective. The objective level in a person's life and in relationships is what we are trying to read in the dreamwork: What is the objective at issue at the moment? True, each person experiences it subjectively. But simply to say, "all knowing is subjective" lames the search for the objectivity that is there and which we may be able to get a partial glimpse of.

Von Franz is trying to express the subtle shift in consciousness that occurs when we go from a three level of consciousness to a four level. In "four" there is a recognition of our subjectivity, but also the knowledge that there is more to life than subjectivity. Three is "I'm right, you're wrong." Four is "Here is my point of view" and "I hear your point of view," *but the question remains concerning the objective perception of the situation from the point of view of the dream.*

In other words, dreams are saying something. We do our best with our subjectivity to get their meaning. But the dream means something whether we have understood it or not. And if we consistently miss the intent of the dream, our physiology reacts. The postmodern point of view works if we exclude the body. But sooner or later the body breaks down if there is a message that doesn't succeed in getting through to us.[90] The unconscious has something very specific to say; that is the objectivity: it has a point of view of its own. Four is the midpoint between its objectivity and our subjectivity. Four represents the ability to dialogue, to at-

---

[90] See Anne Maguire's work.

tempt to approach the truth known by the dream. It is the ability to hear ourselves and to hear the other—in ourselves and "out there."

Though it sounds nearly pedantic to go into these matters, how we conceive of knowing does influence how we understand, and practice, the art of therapy. From experience, we hold that dreams, at least at times, know objectively. True, our knowledge of them is filtered through our personality. The individual quality of knowing, however, does not lead us to be content with subjectivity. Rather, with the conviction of their importance, it spurs us on to seek the dreams' objectivity—of course, always mindful of our penchant for error.

Von Franz's reference to time at the end of the quote pertains to the fact that understanding has to be filtered through and affected by the moment we are living in. The psychological demands of different historical periods are diverse and influence the way we express our inner experience. With four the issue of time is again relevant. The attitude we take to our experience has to be tempered by the demands of the time in which we live. That is also part of this shift to four. The transition from three to four is from certainty (three) to "subjective objectivity" or "objective subjectivity" in dialogue with the character of the historical period (four). Take a simple example of the experience of kindness and its importance. Today there is a ruthlessness loose in daily intercourse that was simply not present thirty or forty years ago. Generosity to the world requires much more circumspection today than it did one or two generations ago, otherwise it will be eaten up by the sociopathic drift of our time.

Levels of Consciousness

Her next paragraphs recap the personality characteristics of each number:

> The numerical rhythms one, two, three and four, described in the last chapter . . . *acquire an especially decisive significance when they appear as the structural characteristics of the Self symbol.* [124]

Numbers are symbols for aspects of the process of coming to consciousness of selfhood; there is nothing new in that sentence. Numbers become bound up with specific psychic attitudes toward reality, which correspond to certain levels of consciousness. [124]

Now she describes typical patterns of behavior which correspond to the different levels of consciousness.

> In his paper on the Trinity,[91] Jung describes the first three of these steps in detail: at the level of one, man still naively participates in his surroundings in a state of uncritical unconsciousness, submitting to things as they are. [124]

I'm sure we can think of a situation when we have been treated unfairly and we do, or are expected to, go along with it. That is the one. There is a conflict, but no seeing. It is wholeness, but it is wholeness without reflection. To go from wholeness without reflection to wholeness with reflection is no small matter.

> At the level of two, on the other hand, a dualistic world- and God-image gives rise to tension, doubt, and criticism of God, life, nature, and oneself. The condition of three by comparison denotes insight, the rise of consciousness, and the rediscovery of unity on a higher level; in a word, gnosis and knowledge. [125]

That is two and three, but next is what is so important in this chapter:

> But no final goal is reached by this step, for "trinitarian" thinking lacks a further dimension: it is flat, intellectual, and consequently encourages intolerant and absolute declarations. [125]

That is the danger of first insights. It is true what we are seeing may have come from an inner insight based on a dream image with clear convincing power. Seemingly objectively true from an inner experience, the insight seems incontrovertible. But it is coming through us, our person, which is subjective. That is why she says:

> The "eternal" character and "absolute validity" of certain archetypal structures is certainly recognized, but ego consciousness assumes the role of their herald. [125]

---

[91] "A Psychological Approach to the Dogma of the Trinity," *Psychology and Religion,* CW 11, pars. 269ff.

Herald there means "spokesperson," "supporter," "mouthpiece," etc.

> From this standpoint one overlooks the fact that although these structures may well be timeless and eternal in the unconscious, they become modified when they make the transition into the field of individual consciousness. [125]

The same ideas in this chapter keep coming back in different ways. An objective fact expressed, as accurately as we are able through our subjective perception, is the business of four.

> By granting absolute validity, within the framework of trinitarian thought, to a realization, we overlook the fact that an element shining forth as a "timeless structure" in the unconscious has been reconstructed through discursive thought processes, and, in this process, became temporally conditioned. [125]

The "objective" when it meets time takes on a garb of the person knowing it and of the times.

> The transition of an unconscious content into our time-bound consciousness involves a diminution of the primal forms simultaneously comprehended, and precisely because of this it is erroneous to evaluate our insights by naïvely attributing eternal validity to them. [125f.]

As has been said, in a dream image there is often an objective read on a situation, but it has to be humanized.

Consciousness Today

> Though we realize the eternal character of a primal intuition in consciousness, we overlook the fact that this realization is a reconstruction reached by way of time-bound discursive mental processes which have no absolute validity. [126]

> Instead of proclaiming absolute dogmas, a "quaternary" attitude of mind then develops which, more modestly, seeks to describe reality in a manner that will—if it is based on an archetypal concept—be understandable to others. One remains simultaneously aware of the fact that assumptions of the unconscious do indeed reflect outer or inner reality, but also that they are transformed, through their passage into consciousness, into constricted, time-bound language. [126]

An ego that is three-bound is pompous and unable to really listen and dialogue. An ego characterized by four is able to consider the point of view of others and to enter into a discussion with them. Selfhood comes when we have learned to listen to ourselves and to listen to others as well.

Von Franz brings these ideas to a close by referring to the medieval Trinitarian Christian viewpoint that tried to ban all darkness and evil from its world picture and which maintained the obstinate conviction of its rightness. In contrast, the shift to four means taking account of darkness and evil, particularly one's own darkness and evil.[92] The birth of humility, the ability to both talk and listen, the capacity to take account of our subjectivity, is a shift carried out not without personal pain:

> It is therefore not surprising that the step from three to four involves particular difficulties for it is bound up with painful insights. [129]

But the pain brings gain, as it leads, perhaps for the first time in our life, to an emotional opening. This is what she refers to by the French, *"une expérience d'ouverture,"* an experience of opening:

> [This] consists in a deepening of realization which . . . no longer involves the summary and brutal coercion of one variant over another. [131]

How much of life is just that? The coercion of one person over another, or the coercion of one point of view over another, is the power game of today. Four is about a different way of living; four leads not to force "but . . . to dialectical synthesis." [131]

That is, four concerns real discussion and mutual consideration of the other's point of view. In the four stage, the dynamic is not power, it is the emergence of true exchange.

The Observer Effect

The attitude of four, in which there is dialogue, is paralleled in quantum physics by its understanding of reality. Each observation for a quantum physicist is, so to speak, a "dialogue" with the object observed. In seeing something, at the very, very small quantum level, the observer has partially determined its character. By looking at it, it has been disturbed.

---

[92] As in the third and fourth floor apartments in chapter 2.

The outlook dominating modern physics, which includes the observer and takes into account such new insights as the irreversibility of measurement acts, is paralleled in psychology by the recognition of the reality of the unconscious and by the serious consideration given to the shadow as well as to the psychic reality of dreams and "numina" (signs) through which synchronistic events manifest themselves. In this way intellectual formulations take on the character of more modest attempts at description, and individual moral responsibility plays a far more significant role in psychological understanding. Insight into the unconscious aspects of one's own personality becomes unavoidable, because "the shadow and the opposing will are the necessary conditions for all actualization," and for every achievement of consciousness as well. [133f.]

Both in physics and psychology we realize the importance of the subject. In physics there is the realization that observations at the subatomic level influence what is being observed, and this must be taken into account as science seeks to create its grasp of reality. In psychology we see repeatedly how the inner journey and its lessons teach us of the fallibility of our judgment—and of the importance of events inside and outside ourselves, for example synchronicities, in guiding our lives. The tyranny of consciousness is dethroned as it learns the importance of inner and synchronistic guidance.

A shift toward the recognition of subjectivity is occurring in tandem within the two disciplines of physics and psychology. Von Franz feels it is very important that science has recognized subjectivity in its worldview. It is the first time science has ever said that the nature of the subject is a factor crucial to understanding. This is the same kind of shift that people are making personally as they move from the three to four phase of developing consciousness. Maybe this is the first time in history that such a development is possible. A development whereby we can both have and detach from our own "divine truth," *and* enter into open conversation and productive self-reflection, is perhaps possible to us for the first time ever.

Personally I find that development the poignant asset of our time.[93]

---

[93] Remember the Axiom of Maria? The four is at the same time the one—a singular, solid, and unique individual who is open.

PART III

The Field of the Collective Unconscious and Its Inner Dynamism

Chapter 8

Archetypes and Numbers as "Fields" of Unfolding Rhythmical Sequences

Part III, chapters 8 and 9, are transitions. Part IV, in chapters 10 and 11, discusses mandalas which are dual. Double mandalas portray in image form the two aspects of life we have just discussed conceptually in terms of numbers: the pattern of our being, which exists as a potential; and the existence of space and time. Chapter 13 probes chances which "happen more often than chance allows," as Jung once put it.[94] Meaningful chance events are those moments in which hints of the pattern of our being manifest in daily living.

Numbers as Fields

Let's look at the first sentence of the chapter:

In modern number theory one speaks of integers in their entirety as a field. [139]

We have heard of "gravitational fields" or "magnetic fields." Take the magnetic field. If I put a magnet under a piece of paper, then sprinkle iron filings on the paper, a pattern is formed by the filings. This happens because a magnetic field is present. A field, we could say loosely, is a continuum of force. Now apply this to numbers. We think, "one, two, three" as if they are separate chunks. But number theory likens numbers to fields. What we think of as one, two, three, etc., are simply points on a continuum of numerical values, discrete stops along the way. The

---

[94] Richard Evans, *Jung on Elementary Psychology*, p. 143.

mathematician means this in a literal way, while von Franz's purpose is to appraise the psychological validity of the mathematical statement. In this she has returned to her point in chapter 2 (numbers as qualities, as symbols) and chapter 4 (numbers are various expressions of the one continuum).

Hence she writes:

> This concept of a field or structure appears to me to be applicable, in another form, to an aspect of the qualitative one-continuum. [141][95]

Numbers are a flow of gradation of amount. Again to the nonmathematician this statement may sound like gibberish. Why even bring it up? Because psychologically, it makes a lot of sense. Here is an example to illustrate.

An Example

I once was working with a married fellow who felt conflicted about his attraction to pornography. One day I asked him to consider what he would be doing if he weren't looking at his collection of pictures. I suggested that sometime when he felt like looking at pornography he just sit quietly and see if any other desires came into his mind. He meditated on this for several months, and then reported that playing war games with toy soldiers was what he felt like doing. So at my encouragement he built a sandbox, played with metal toy soldiers, and even began making them by learning the rudiments of casting metal.

That went on for quite a while, about a year. Soon he began to study war battles and reenact them in his sandbox with these toy soldiers. When I, some months later, again addressed this issue, I asked what it was that he found so exciting about playing with toy soldiers. He thought about this question again for some months. He then said that his toy interest had led him into a fascination with history; he found studying the history of these battles, and the historical context of the wars he was reenacting, captivating. To make a long story short, over time the toy war

---

[95] She continues the discussion of numbers as fields on pages 144-147.

games subsided, and he developed an interest in history itself. He began searching out and collecting original photographs of the particular period in history that had come to fascinate him, and soon made quite an extensive exhibit of photographs of this period of American history. He took that exhibit to various venues where it was displayed and was well received. He then reported to me that the desire for pornography had gone by the wayside.

An Interpretation

Now consider the above example from my practice in light of von Franz mentioning that numbers are all different expressions of the one continuum, that numbers are fields of gradation which "surface" at points as discrete integers.

The man's interest went from a *first* stage of interest in pornography to a *second* stage of interest in toy soldiers and war games to a *third* interest of studying the historical background of certain battles and of the period of history in which they occurred, to a *fourth* stage of an interest in history for its own sake, at which time the original interest had transformed. This *transformation of his interest through different stages* occurred over the course of several years. It was not the main focus of our therapy; conversations about daily issues, etc., took up much more of our time. His change occurred almost at the subterranean level; we referred to it only from time to time when he reported his hunches to me. These ideas were presented to him more than "thought out." Then for months at a time he worked on his own at the projects his hunches thus suggested. So his interest evolved naturally from an initial state through a final state, with him just following up on his unfolding curiosity.

Note how clearly the first interest evolved over a sequence of stages. It is this sequential aspect of development that relates psychology so intimately to number symbolism. The second stage, then, was another form of his original interest, just changed; the third stage was another form of his second interest, just changed; and the fourth stage was another form of the third stage, just changed. Each stage was a *different qualitative expression of the interest in the previous stage*, and, by extension, the final stage of his interest in history was a different qualitative expression of his original fascination with pornography. It was the same interest in him that changed through different states to its final form. That is what von Franz means by her psychological interpretation of the mathematical statement that numbers are different forms of the one-continuum. In the case of this man, the different states of his interest were different forms of his original one.[96] And this is also an example of what she means by the psychological interpretation of the mathematical statement that numbers are specific points along the way of a number field.

In the case of the man, his interest went from pornography to history in a process of gradual transformation which appeared as specific new interests along the way. But these specific, interim interests were simply moments in his life when the gradual process of change from pornography fascination to historical creativity were evident in a particular aspect. This is critical to Jungian therapy because we try to understand certain "pathological"-appearing personality traits as unformed conditions of an as-yet unrealized future development. It wasn't that there was something "wrong" with the appeal pornography had for him. It was that the appeal held an undeveloped, unfinished form of his future interest in history. It just needed the chance to finish its development, and that was part of the job of the analytic process. Our task was, so to speak, to become aware of his "one-continuum," of that one part of him that wanted to evolve through several stages, of that one part of him that would evolve gradually as if it were a field, appearing along the way in several intermediate states, until it reached its final goal.

When we can visualize an example of the sometimes abstract-sounding mathematical statements in *Number and Time*, their psychological relevance becomes clearer. The effect on a life of an understood process of sequential transformation from the inside out is astonishing. What could better attest to the magnitude of von Franz's work?

---

[96] His fantasies in pornography became fancifully playful games; the fancifully playful games became an interest in history which was both fanciful and playful; the fancifully playful historical interest became a creative interest in history. At each stage there was a contribution to the expanding interest which was preserved in the final interest. In that sense each new interest "contained" the previous forms and was a synthesis of them.

Number and Spirit

We have been able to see an example of how there is an inner guidance to the personality. The man did not sit down and think, "Now I am going to do this and then this" and so on. The various interests that evolved *occurred* to him as half intuitions, half feelings, in something like fantasy states. This inborn (recall Jung's conclusions by 1928) capacity for inner guidance that can move life forward along a meaningful line is another way to express the Jungian understanding of *spirit*, a term which I talked about and gave a provisional definition of in chapter 3. Here von Franz revisits that definition again as the archetype of order which is symbolized by numbers:

> Jung defines natural number as the archetype of order which has become conscious. [143]

And

> This inborn disposition engenders the knowledge and rational formulations of order which we experience in consciousness. [143]

She has reminded us again of the link between spirit, number, and order.[97]

Story and Number

A story is a sequential series of events. The scenes are not arbitrary steps. For example, what sense would it convey to have Ophelia commit suicide *before* her father was killed by Hamlet? First comes Hamlet's killing of her father, and then, second, comes Ophelia's despair and suicide. So number is implicitly present in stories. That is why we have plays of several acts. Number is the structural sequence of anything, whether images or stories or dreams. Hence von Franz calls numbers "typical phases

---

[97] In presenting this material in workshops, I have encountered the objection that "order" sounds so neat, clean and logical, so unlike life. If the word strikes us that way, substitute "meaningful unfolding" or "a feeling I am getting somewhere in life." Her use of the word order does not ignore the reality of chaos and, but it emphasizes the importance of finding our way forward in life. In our example of the man, he moved forward from pornography to history.

of narration." [150] She adds: "Stories may be described as *temporal number sequences*." [153]

The next chapter will pick up the theme of sequence from yet another point of view. It will survey how Jung understood that life can move forward by way of inner images. And wait till you hear what a lovely psychoanalytic society contributed to my presentation of our budding historian and his pictures.

Chapter 9

Numbers as Isomorphic Configurations of Motion in Psychic and Physical Energy

Jung's Concept of Energy

To appreciate the next chapter it will be necessary first to review Jung's concept of psychic energy. We have seen the purposive activity of the unconscious as conflict seeks resolution, and we have seen it in the example of a man's developing interest in history. Like the motion of matter at the subatomic level, the psyche has a capacity to move forward along a course of action only it seems to know ahead of time. In all of this Jung saw the transformation of energy, and he clarified his views in a particularly interesting essay, "On Psychic Energy."[98] We will look at that essay briefly because it spells out the nature of psychological change which Jung alone recognized and delineated.

> It is a generally recognized truth that physical events can be looked at in two ways: from the mechanistic and from the energic standpoint. The mechanistic view is purely causal; it conceives an event as the effect of a cause, in the sense that unchanging substances change their relation to one another according to fixed laws.[99]

There are two perspectives from which to grasp psychological events. Some events have a cause, and some events have a purpose. The mechanistic point of view was the fruit of Freud's work, and the purposive/energic point of view the fruit of Jung's.

What is the mechanistic (also called the causal or reductive) view? I discussed the man I described in the last chapter with a psychoanalytic society which had invited me to present at one of its monthly meetings. The position they brought forth in response to my commentary was that the man's problems could not possibly have been resolved because

---

[98] In *The Structure and Dynamics of the Psyche*, CW 8, pars. 1ff.

[99] Ibid., par. 2.

"studies showed" that sexual deviance is linked to repressed hostility. They then attacked me for not having dealt with the man's anger. I said, "He wasn't particularly angry." "Oh, yes, he was," they said, *"because studies have shown* that sexual deviancy is definitely linked to repressed hostility. Sexual deviancy is an expression of anger." They continued their response by pointing out that we can see the man's anger in his choice of war games; and I had not dealt with that, they claimed. The reason he played with toy soldiers was that they were a covert expression of the anger from some unresolved event in childhood.

That is the causal point of view. The "unchanging substance," for them, was the anger which (they said) went unacknowledged from childhood to adulthood, from an event in childhood to pornography in adulthood; and the aggression hidden in his pornographic interest subsequently surfaced in his war games. His pornography interests and his playing war with toy soldiers was *caused* by the anger from childhood.

What about the energic (also called the final or purposive[100]) point of view?

> The energic point of view on the other hand is in essence final . . . . The flow of energy has a definite direction (goal) in that it follows the gradient of potential in a way that cannot be reversed. The idea of energy is not that of a substance moved in space [the anger mentioned above]; it is a concept abstracted from relations of movement.[101]

The energic point of view doesn't see a chain of events going from past *to* present, it sees a chain of events in which a future state is seeking to evolve *from* the present. (Figure 13) In the energic point of view it is the end state, the interest in history, that has a prior meaning or that is a potentiality waiting to be realized within the personality. There is a natural gradient of energy which first surfaces in childhood and then presses *toward its final form* through various configurations along the way. It is only when that movement is thwarted somehow that it becomes problematic. Past events are means whereby the energy, heading for its final

---

[100] Sometimes "teleological" is also used to characterize this viewpoint, meaning "goal directed." *Telos* is Greek for goal.

[101] *The Structure and Dynamics of the Psyche,* CW 8, par. 3.

The past causes the present

The past "pushes" the present

The present seeks the future

The future "pulls" the present

Figure 13. Causality vs. purpose.

goal, finds temporary expressions until it reaches its goal. In the case of our historian, it was not able to move forward to its final goal because there were no tools in consciousness to understand it;[102] his psychic energy then got stuck and surfaced in the form of pornography. Recall my assertion that the pornography interest was not an indication there was something wrong with this man; but rather it indicated there was something right with him (the final interest in history) that had, at the time of his beginning therapy, no way to reach its final goal. The future potential is the accomplishment that the personality is in the process of trying to

---

[102] At times recourse to the past is helpful in understanding how the future was blocked, but for this man such inquiry yielded very little. In any case, when it is a question of the purposive movement of the psyche, the past cannot explain the specific character of the present, though it can be part of what keeps the future at bay.

bring to completion. The unlived potential (what we have called the transcendental continuum, for example) is what is primary, and there is a dynamic in the unconscious which seeks to bring that into reality. It *arranges* what it needs to come into being. In working with such a person the therapist is asking him or herself, "What is the end state that this person's energy is moving toward?" When we see what looks like pathology, we ask, "How is this an incomplete expression of something that is seeking realization? What is the potential end state?"

It is important to note that Jung recognizes the truth in both these points of view. But it is a question of knowing when to utilize which approach.[103] There are times when the events in our life are caused and there are times when events are purposed. I wouldn't want to be understood as saying that everything is purposed, but in this case I stuck to my guns that "goal-directed" was the way to understand the man's growth—not that it mattered to our "psychoanalysts," because "studies showed …"[104] They were adamantly stuck in three-thinking.

It was in our man's given potential to become involved in history. Furthermore it is when the psyche is trying to move to the future from the present, though the movement may seem like a "pathological" state of the personality, that numbers are likely to appear in dreams and fantasies as compelling symbols. Numbers are not as important symbolically when we are dealing with causes. But when the energic or purposive point of view comes into play, numbers are likely to appear meaningfully in our dreamscape.

Another sentence from Jung's essay merits attention: "What to the causal view is fact to the final [or energic] view is *symbol.*"[105]

The causal view, expressed in the psychoanalytic protest to my presentation, saw the various stages of the man's growth, the pictures, the toys, the war-games, etc., as facts of his life. I, working from the energic

---

[103] That is the art of the analytic work.

[104] How refreshing is Jung: "If I want to understand an individual human being, I must lay aside all scientific knowledge of the average man and discard all theories in order to adopt a completely new and unprejudiced attitude." ("The Undiscovered Self," *Civilization in Transition*, CW 10, par. 495)

[105] "On Psychic Energy," *The Structure and Dynamics of the Psyche*, CW 8, par. 45.

point of view, saw them each as symbols, part expressions of a future accomplishment that contained all of the interests of this man which surfaced along the way. Those various manifestations pointed toward, were hints of, his future self. In other words, they were symbols. Those events in his life were symbolic expressions of the goal of his inwardly transforming personality. If we recall Jung's understanding of spirit, this next sentence of Jung's provides a nice summing up the contrast between two ways of looking at psychological development that he delineated. In the causal point of view,

> the spiritual principle is not recognized as an equivalent counterpart of the instincts.[106]

When the spirit is pulling us forward through the various stages of our life until we fulfill our potential, it is vital to be sensitive to the qualitative role of numbers in the psyche.

Motion Patterns

Von Franz discusses the relation of numbers to psychic energy because it is when the psyche is growing in a purposive way that numbers are most likely to appear symbolically in dreams.

She sums up the main point of the chapter near its end. Natural number is

> the common ordering factor of both physical and psychic manifestations of energy, and is consequently the element that draws psyche and matter together. In other words, amorphous energy probably does not exist at all; when energy manifests itself in either psychic or physical dimensions, it is always "numerically" structured . . . . Natural numbers appear to represent the typical, universally recurring, common motion patterns of both psychic *and* physical energy. Because these motion patterns (number) are identical for both forms of energy, the human mind can, on the whole, grasp the phenomena of the outer world. [166]

She draws our attention to the similar understanding of energy as physical

---

[106] Ibid., par. 104.

energy in physics and as psychological energy in our personality. She refers to numbers as describing motion patterns (motion indicates energy). In physics that would be the fact that, at the subatomic level, electrons can move in only certain numerically patterned orbits. In psychology that refers to numbers symbolically portraying the movement of psychological growth. Moreover, she concludes by stating that it is by virtue of this parallelism in numerical forms between matter and psyche that we can conceive of the laws of science.

Got Rhythm?

Number and rhythm, what is the relationship and why does von Franz mention it? Looking anthropologically at the first indications of the human species' ability to transform energy in the way we have discussed, she says that it is in rhythmic back and forth motions that early peoples began to focus raw instinct into more disciplined activity. She cites rock art to show how the lines of very early (Paleolithic = Old Stone Age) art were made by inscribing on the rock in a back and forth motion. [160f.] So the first capacity to transform energy, the very initial harnessing of energy at one level and transforming it to another, as we saw in a very refined form in the pornography example, surfaced in early human society in the rhythm of back and forth. This is how number first appeared in its transformative capability during the evolution of the human species: in the two of the back and forth rhythm.

On pages 162-163 she recounts the dream of a theologian which contains a striped pattern as an example of the back and forth theme indicating the possibility of change. It is when we can follow this gradient of our lives consciously and make our potential (the first, primal unity of potential—present but undeveloped) a reality that we have the experience of living meaningfully. Her discussion continues through page 166.

Chapter Summary

Chapter 9 finishes part III. Chapter 8 returned to the notion of numbers as symbols. Chapter 9 provided another glimpse into the faculty of the psyche to create our story, step-by-step, from within. Number as symbol has, of course, been important in all of this.

Part IV now examines from a fresh vantage point the two dimensions that make up a meaningful life. Meaningful living, we could say, occurs in stereo. The left channel is the realm of potential with an inner dynamic for realization; the right channel is time and space where that potential seeks to take root. Putting number symbolism aside for a moment, we will now take a look at the "two-part" aspect of existence from the point of view of mandalas that are double.

PART IV

Historical and Mathematical Models of the *Unus Mundus*

Chapter 10

Historical Mandala Models as Inner Psychic Equivalents of the *Unus Mundus*

Double mandalas depict, on the one hand, their tradition's view of the heavenly sphere of life, and, on the other, their tradition's view of the earthly sphere of life. In this chapter von Franz explores several cultures' images which illustrate that wholeness consists of two parts. In these examples, two circles go to make up the objects of meditation on the unity of life. She examines the double images as metaphors to illustrate her thesis that it takes an awareness of two dimensions of life to make it significant.

There is much amplification material in the chapter,[107] and it will suffice to familiarize ourselves with one of her examples. For those who are dream interpreters, a familiarity with the many specifics in the chapter will prove rewarding, but for other readers an overall appreciation of the image form will be enough. Since the theme has such a guiding presence in dreams, I will also explore several dreams where the mandala which is two appears significantly.

The *Unus Mundus*

Von Franz revisits the concept of the *unus mundus* because it is the "one" that the dual mandala expresses in doubled form.

---

[107] Amplification provides the mythological context of an image so we can see, as an aid to understanding its meaning, how the image has appeared in different cultural or religious traditions.

Jung used the expression *unus mundus* to designate the transcendental unitary reality underlying the dualism of psyche and matter. [171]

And recall synchronicity is the one moment in which we see the unitary reality of psyche and matter. It is the moment when the physical world and the dream world act the same way. Remember, too, that the *unus mundus* has been used in two senses, as we have seen in chapter 1.

Here is another statement of the first of the two:

The expression *unus mundus* originated in medieval natural philosophy, where it denoted the timeless, preexistent, cosmic plan or antecedent world model, potential in God's mind. [171]

That is putting in theological language what we have called the continuum of preexistent possibility. She then cites Joannes Scotus Erigena, a ninth-century Irish theologian. He refers to the preexistent, cosmic plan by which God created the universe as Wisdom [or Sophia, in Greek]. Erigena writes that Wisdom represents

the primal original forms which not only lie in God, but constitute God Himself. [172]

For Erigena what we are calling the transcendental continuum has been ascribed to the mind of God. Von Franz is not addressing whether the transcendental continuum is God or not. What interests her is how many people have had the same idea of a transcendental dimension which creates life by coming into daily events. In any case, von Franz's citations bring very attractive mention of Wisdom or Sophia into the analysis, but further consideration of her lies outside our present scope.[108]

Von Franz continues Erigena's remarks:

These "causae primordiales" [primal original forms or causes] know themselves. [172]

That is an interesting phrase. What does it mean? It is like there is not only a pattern of who we are preexistent to us; this pattern is not a simply the knowledge of who we are to be, it is actually a knowing, a sentient

---

[108] For a brief overview of Sophia in this regard see *At the Heart of Matter*, pp. 147ff. Also von Franz's *Aurora Consurgens* is a magnificent treatise on Sophia.

knower; it is a living entity inside of us. There is an intelligence in the knowing that is apart from our ego intelligence. There is a consciousness in us that knows us.

The second use of the word *unus mundus* is an extension of its first sense. She refers to the view of the medieval alchemists:

> They did not only conceive of the *unus mundus* as the initial plan of the universe existing in God's mind; for them it was also identical with the goal they were seeking, the *lapis*. It, like the *res simplex* [= the simple thing, another word for the goal] or the philosophers' stone, was the *one* world. According to Parcelsus' pupil, Gerhard Dorn, the highest grade of the alchemical *coniunctio* [or union] consisted in the union of the total man with the *unus mundus*. [173]

The last sentence, "the union of the total man with the *unus mundus*," replays our understanding of the spirit-matter unity. Recall that some alchemists thought that when gold was created in the alchemical vessel, the effects of that gold emanated from the vessel. They also felt that the effects emanated *from within the alchemist*, outward to and through the world.[109] Psychologically speaking, when we have achieved an awareness of ourselves there will be an effect on the environment and/or community around us. A synchronicity is a prime example of where the inner world reproduces itself in the outer world, at that particular moment there is a unity between inside and outside. That is the other sense of the *unus mundus*.

Von Franz refers to Jung's summing up the two uses of the term:

> Jung . . . stresses the fact that he views the unitary reality underlying synchronstic phenomena as a "potential" reality "in so far as all those conditions which determine the form of empirical phenomena are inherent to it."[110] The phenomena of synchronicity ... represent sporadic actualizations of this unitary world. [173f.]

---

[109] Gerhard Dorn, in particular. Dorn was a sixteenth-century alchemist. See *Mysterium Coniunctionis*, CW 14, part VI. See also Edward F. Edinger, *The Mysterium Lectures*, chapters 23-25.

[110] *Mysterium Coniunctionis*, par.769.

She began the chapter with this discussion as background to the dual mandala since they portray the unity which is two.

Examples of Dual Mandalas

A variety of examples are offered for our consideration, from Jung's *Aion*[111] through to China, ancient Greece, Neoplatonism, early alchemy, Gnosticism, the Middle Ages, and on to modern physics. I have picked one example to illustrate common elements.

An elegant representative of the series is the diagram on page 176. (Figure 14) The picture is from the Cabbala, the center of mystical Judaism. The Cabbalist's image of God is characterized by God's ten manifestations or Sephiroth.[112] In the diagram they are the circles within the topmost circle. That tenfold character of God as the encompassing circle is then manifest on earth in ten different ways. They are represented in the lower circles underneath the larger, upper circle. The correspondence between the large upper "container" circle and the bottom circles

> would *illustrate the effective emanations of the Primal One throughout the various realms of nature.* [177, emphasis added]

So there is the dual mandala: God in heaven, God as present in emanations in the world. This is understood as metaphor for the timeless and the time-bound. A primal presence intermingles with life on earth.

Dreams

I would like to examine four dreams. One she quotes in the chapter, the other three are from my analytic practice.

Wolfgang Pauli's dream which she relates on page 184 is a classic in the Jungian literature.[113] Its main features mark it as an image of the dual

---

[111] CW 9ii, chap. 14. See also Edward Edinger, *The Aion Lectures*, chaps. 22-24.

[112] "Sephirot," Wikipedia.

[113] "Individual Dream Symbolism in Relation to Alchemy," CW 12, pars. 307ff. and "Psychology and Religion," CW 11, pars. 111ff. See also Lindorff, *Pauli and Jung: The Meeting of Two Great Minds*, pp. 44ff., and my *At the Heart of Matter*, pp. 139ff.

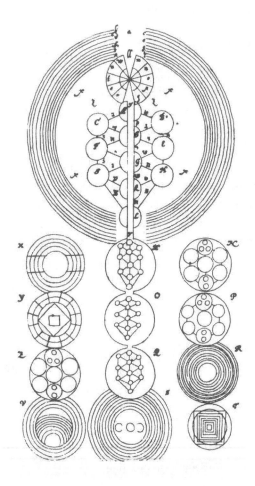

Figure 14. The Cabalistic *Sefiroth* Tree.

mandala. (Figure 15) In the dream there are two colorful intersecting circles, a vertical and a horizontal one, making up the "world clock." The
rhythms of the pointers on each clock are then specified.

Figure 15. Wolfgang Pauli's World Clock.

For our purposes, the important characteristic of the dream is the two circles. The vertical circle is blue, the color of the expanse from the oceans to the heavens. It aptly symbolizse the transcendental dimension which then intersects the earthly, horizontal circle of four colors. Pauli had the dream when he was in his thirties during his personal crisis evidenced by alcoholism, cynicism, and obnoxious behavior. In such a state of mind a person is not likely to hold that there is any transcendent dimension to life and is likely to treat life as an arena for pleasure and self-aggrandizement. The dream was showing Pauli that there *is* a greater pattern to life. Part of the solution to his debauchery would be to begin attuning himself to the greater pattern and to live from the more comprehensive sense of himself.

The second example comes from a woman approaching midlife. She was quite successful professionally but had begun to feel bored. The feeling of boredom and meaninglessness contrasted sharply to what she knew she had achieved. At the top of her profession, she had a satisfactory marriage, and was comfortable financially. Here is her dream:

> There are two circles. In the first circle there was a fire that had burnt down and left a colored ash of something that resembled spices. It wasn't just gray ash, it was a dark-green color, like spices. There is nothing in the other circle. On the right hand side was the fire, on the left hand side was nothing.

The burnt down state of the first circle would represent the destruction of her previous sense of what was important in life. Only ash is left of that phase of her life. The prior phase of her life is over but the next has not yet started. That is why she feels so rotten. What about the other circle? It is a void, but likely portrays the place where the transcendental continuum can be met. She has lost her orientation (the right circle), but the pattern of the real self awaits discovery in the left circle. That is yet potentially available to her to reorient her, though she had no idea of it at the moment: hence the emptiness of the circle. So the work of her analysis is first to delve into and to bring up who she is, to get an image of who she is, from the now-empty left-hand circle. Then her task will be to construct that figure in the right-hand circle of daily life.

When the figure is constructed in the right-hand circle, the potential of the next phase of her life will be made real, which will replace what the fire has burnt down. The possibility of a positive outcome is indicated by the green, herb-like color of the ash. We know from the dual mandala that the sense of meaningful living comes when what is in the left-hand circle of potential is being lived in the right-hand circle of day-to-day— in other words, when the inborn potential of genuine selfhood is constructed in time and space. All of this is implied and conveyed in the two circles in the dream, an example of the dual mandala theme and its portrayal of life's two dimensions.

The two-circled mandala appears again in a dream of a woman who experienced serious belittlement as a child and was working to recover her self-esteem:

There are two spheres which appear in the dream. The first looks something like the yin/yang symbol. [Figure 16] It is black and white and seems to be the profile of an old woman on the white side. I wasn't able to discern what the other shape was, but it would have been the complement of the old woman's profile. The second image was similar to the first, but the type of design was more like Art Deco, more straight lines, shiny.

Figure 16. The Chinese Taijitu diagram (yin-yang symbol).

The dreamer reported that she did not particularly like Art Deco, finding its shiny lines fake and unreal. That would represent the dreamer's sense of herself in adulthood. She reported how she had always been persecuted as a child for her genuine emotions and points of view. She had been taught to withhold her true reactions and to feel she was of no value. In contrast to her "denuded" Art Deco sense of herself, the dual mandala theme shows her an image of the potential to real selfhood. It is a portrait of authentic womanhood, a mixture of light and dark, waiting for her to develop. While she could rightly feel sorry that early life had given her such a crummy deal—what has a child ever done to deserve such treatment?—the present held the possibility of creating new strength and value, personified in the second circle. Her potential genuine self was still waiting to be developed as shown by the image in the other half of the double mandala.

The final dream comes from a woman with considerable artistic talent who was seeking to find its expression consistent with her interests and values.

> The key to my car is made up of 2 circles that hook together. I start the car and begin trying to drive it but strange things begin to happen: the car changes form, and it will not respond to my attempts to control it. Finally I arrive and I try to remove the keys from the ignition, but they are soft and they break off in the switch. Once the car is parked, a man smashes into my car—damaging the body. He tries to escape without paying for the damages. I physically grab hold of him and force him to the ground. He is a junk collector and offers to pay for the damage by giving me junk instead of cash. I insist on being paid cash.

In the dream, the dual mandala is not yet a firm idea: the two circles are soft. The firm conviction that we have the right to know who we are, and to bring that into life is the dreamer's current challenge. When she tries to grasp her birthright, the battle with the feeling that "I am junk" starts; such is the contention that tries to destroy the dreamer's car, that is, her ability to move forward. The man does not succeed because the dreamer is determined not to let the feeling of being trash prevail. Indeed, there were elements in the woman's past which could explain this battle to recognize the reality of the right to be. I have also found that anyone who tries to live a creative life in real time and space must go through such a battle.

Every negative voice in the world, whether we have had a cruel or a supportive upbringing, raises its head as soon as we try to do something truly creative.[114] In any case, the notion that life is made up of two di-

---

[114] "Everything that is beyond the ordinary is paid for." (Jung, *Nietzsche's* Zarathustra, p. 197)

mensions, whether it had yet been clarified in the dreamer's consciousness or not, was implanted within her. Her tenacity with the junk man shows her willingness to fight for what she is learning about herself—indeed about life itself and what it can become. The dream is pertinent because of the way it shows that the double circle theme, which sounds pat in theory, forms the foundation on which meaningful living grows and involves a struggle which, at times, draws on the sum total of our resources.

Four dreams of the dual mandala, and they all convey the same: the Self "appears to *consist of two heterogeneous systems* which stand in a functional relationship to each other." [184]

Synchronicity

Von Franz again refers to synchronicity on page 190:

> At the same time, such synchronistic events appear to be linked up with an individual's inner development and in some way dependent on it.

I touched on this passage as a follow up to the last-mentioned dream. Within a few weeks of having the soft-key dream, the woman was put in a position that could have caused a severe, perhaps fatal, automobile accident. While driving on the Interstate and passing a semi, she suddenly encountered a large piece of lumber in the lane directly in front of her. She hit it and the car swerved dangerously, with her almost losing control of it. She said, "I hung onto the steering wheel for dear life." If the car had lost traction and started to spin, she would likely have collided with the tractor-trailer. Then, not too long after the near accident, she was parked in the street outside a friend's house when the neighbor across the street from her friend backed his truck out of the driveway impetuously, and unwittingly smashed into the side of her car causing damage into the thousands of dollars.

Synchronicities indeed. The experience of the synchronicities was very painful, though their message was to be a helpful one. They reminded her that there were forces in life determined to stop her from becoming what she could be. In that way the dream, and the synchronistic events that echoed it, made the point to her, and to anyone who seeks to live their true creative gifts, just how serious the battle for self-expression is and how mindful we must be of the dangerous forces that fear change. Ultimately that destructive voice is inside us, though often its destructiveness can attack from the outside in the actions and words of others. When it comes to creative development, nothing can be taken for granted. We must not only believe in our right to express our gifts, we have also to guard vigilantly against everything, whether inside or outside, that would obliterate it. That was the message the calamities with the automobile conveyed to the woman.

Physics

The chapter ends with a consideration of a conflict in modern physics in light of the dual mandala imagery. The two contemporary models of reality in physics, the relativity theory of Einstein and the Copenhagen Interpretation of Quantum Mechanics, are in direct conflict with each other. Both are accurate in their own domains of analysis, relativity at the level of the universe and motion on a large scale, quantum mechanics at the level of subatomic action and interaction. But Einstein's theory is deterministic and does not admit the validity of "chance" occurrences, as does quantum mechanics. Einstein could never accept the implications of atomic physics that there is randomness at the heart of matter.[115] Von Franz's footnote 60 on page 190 gives the most succinct explication of the disagreement between Einstein (the "relativists") and the quantum physicists:

> The determinism of general relativity theory stands in a certain (complementary) antithesis to quantum theory which, as a result of Heisenberg's uncertainty principle, admits of a certain freedom.

---

[115] Hence his famous statement that God does not play dice. (A. Calaprice, ed., *The Expanded Quotable Einstein*, p. 245.) I wonder if Einstein knew of Krishna's statement in *The Bhagavad-Gita*, "I am the game of dice." (*The Bhagavad-Gita*, p. 94.) See page 225 in *Number and Time* for further mention of God's dice.

The uncertainty principle is the work of Werner Heisenberg, one of the final cofounders of quantum physics along with Niels Bohr and Wolfgang Pauli. Heisenberg's contribution to the physical theory involves our inability to know and predict motion at the subatomic level with full accuracy. It is the aspect of quantum mechanics that recognizes the existence of chance at the micro-level. Einstein's theory does not want to admit the validity of chance as "the way things are" in physics; quantum theory sees chance as a basic principle of "the way things are."

Von Franz mentions this in light of the double mandala theme because several physicists have tried to address the absence of chance (and hence the possibility of meaningful chance) in Einstein's relativity theory by saying that his theory is not a complete description of reality. They felt a need to posit another "dimension" to it:

> The French physicist Olivier Costa de Beauregard recently attributed an additional psychic aspect to the relativistic [i.e., Einstein's] world model. He emphasizes that "the Universe explored by physicists is not the entirety . . . from it the existence of another, far more primordial *psychic* universe may be surmised, of which the material Universe only represents a passive and partial double." [192]

The dual or double theme creeps back in once again. Where the data and calculations of hard relativity science suggest only the existence of predictable events in time and space, the soul of science reacts and posits— in one of its articulate voices—a second, psychic dimension to coexist with matter.

Chapter 11

Divinatory, Mnemotechnical, and Cybernetic Mandalas

We have just talked about dual mandalas from the transcendental side. Chapter 11 considers their earthly side. The previous chapter looked at one side of the mandala pair to represent bringing (transcendental) potential into time and space. This one examines the other side of the mandala pair to represent the capacity for reading the personal quality of a moment in time and space. That quality would reflect what aspect of our larger pattern is present at a given time. She explores the assumption that it is possible to register with oracular means the quality of a moment in time as it reflects the transcendental pattern of our lives. Chapter 10 delved into the transcendental becoming the specific. Chapter 11 probes how the specific conveys knowledge of the transcendental.

What Is Going On Now?

Von Franz begins the chapter by noting the correspondence between the *unus mundus*, its portrayal in mandalas, and its presence in time and space as a synchronicity. She then focuses the chapter on the relation between moments in time as they reflect, and can inform us of, our larger pattern of life. So she refers to the attempts throughout history "to investigate the quality of a specific moment of time." [195]

In the previous chapter we talked about the transcendental continuum "dropping down" into time and space; an oracle, on the other hand, is an attempt to "reach up" into the transcendental world and examine its condition at a particular moment of time. In other words, the investigation of the quality of a specific moment seeks to know what is required of us in *this* moment, what is going on in our lives in *this* moment, when seen from the point of view of our destined potential. The question the investigation of a moment of time by oracular means endeavors to answer concerns about what is going on *now* in its relation to the unfolding and meaning of our lives.

The most familiar system to read the meaning of a moment in time is the horoscope.[116] In the horoscope there is a chart (a circle) thought to be a reflection of the pattern of the heavens (another circle). With that chart we are saying to the transcendental, in effect, "show me your pattern and what it is doing now, so I know how to live, what decisions to make in this moment." The way von Franz puts it is that these divinatory dual mandalas serve as the basis for inquiries into specific "What should I do now? What is going on now?" questions.

She proceeds, through page 198, to look at several dual mandala representations which have been used from earlier times in divinatory reads of a moment's quality. I am not going to attend to these details for the same reason I did not look at all the various examples of the dual mandala in the previous chapter. Mention of the horoscope has given us an introductory sense of the dual mandala in its role as oracle or tool of divination. For the rest of the chapter I will consider her reflections on time as a qualitative factor in its relation to knowledge.

The Individual Confrontation

I draw attention to a statement on page 199, where von Franz says

> that qualitative, specific time moments only emerge out of a latent, undifferentiable continuum *when an individual confronts the continuum.* [199, emphasis added]

The transcendental continuum is only going to yield a meaningful relationship to time when we pay attention to it. That is how I understand, "when an individual confronts the continuum."

If we try to describe what synchronicity is to people they sometimes say, "Well, I never have had any such experiences." But we don't know a special moment of time until we see it. And we don't see it until we know something of what our inner story is that the outer world is trying

---

[116] She is not trying to convince anyone of the validity of astrology. She is observing that there has always been an emotional need to query time, which presupposes a perceived link between the two "systems" represented by the dual mandala. Certainly synchronicity shows us that there are special moments of time, so she seeks historical precedents of this idea.

to reflect back to us. The correspondence between inner and outer will only register if we pay attention to it and make the effort to understand them both. If we don't know our inner world and don't pay attention to the outer world with psychological awareness, we will never be in a position to grasp the meaning of the qualitatively different moments of time in our lives.

Absolute Knowledge

For my tastes, the engaging part of the chapter starts on page 199:

> These [oracular or divinatory] attempts, absurd as they may seem to us today, were directed toward solving a problem which is still unsolved, namely, the fact that *the unconscious actually appears to contain a kind of "knowledge" which is not identical with ego consciousness*. [emphasis added]

The ego is not the only one "in" ourselves that knows what is going on in our lives, and perhaps even in the wider world. We saw an allusion to this in the "causae primordiales" that know themselves. Here she expands that preliminary discussion considerably:

> In his paper "On the Nature of the Psyche," Jung took great pains to demonstrate that the archetypes of the unconscious possess a kind of "quasi intelligence" which is not the same as our ego consciousness.[117]

There is a knowledge within the symbol-creating capacity of the psyche that is independent of our conscious knowledge. Accordingly, we have perceived that the archetype is not limited to the psyche since "inner" images appear in the outer world in synchronicities.

> Jung applied the term "luminosity" to this quasi consciousness of the archetypes, in order to differentiate it from the "light" of ego consciousness.

We associate knowledge with ourselves, "we know"; but Jung holds that there is knowledge that exists apart from "us," the knower in the usual sense of the term. Otherwise how could dreams and synchronicities

---

[117] *The Structure and Dynamics of the Psyche*, CW 8, par. 388.

communicate to us an understanding of our lives which we don't consciously possess?

> The same phenomenon can be observed from another angle when a synchronistic occurrence takes place. Inner and outer facts then behave as if[118] their meaningful relation were *in some way known, but not to our personal consciousness.* [199, emphasis added]

Now that is a complicated statement. Let's look at it. I even hesitate to put the question, because it sounds so silly. But it isn't silly; the problem is that we have no real accepted vocabulary for discussing this point. So here goes. In the two synchronicities that I mentioned at the beginning, how did the letter "know" to be there when I needed it? How did the book at Barnes and Noble "know" to be there for the dreamer? The fact that the outer world is there in a way that we need at a particular moment leads us to ask what the nature of the outer world is that it can resonate with our inner state of mind *at just the right moment.*

It is *as if* something in the synchronistic events I recounted knew what was going on. That is what struck Jung. It is what he called "absolute knowledge." [200] He doesn't want to say that the letter and the book chatted over breakfast, planning to be where I and my analysand needed them, but yet somehow it is as if there were an intelligence in their being there. So knowledge is not something that belongs to our conscious ego, the organ that we normally think of as what understands. It is *as if* some sort of consciousness exists also in events themselves. That is "absolute knowledge." Knowledge, for Jung, isn't something only human beings have. We don't know exactly how to express this, yet elements of events occur together—my confusion and the letter, the man and the book—in a way that defeats probability.

Von Franz continues, stressing the relation between this inner and outer:

> Inner and outer facts then behave as if their meaningful relation were in some way known. [199]

---

[118] Note very carefully that she says "as if." Indeed, von Franz emphasizes throughout *Number and Time* that her work is preliminary and not definitive.

The new challenge that synchronicity brings to the question of knowledge is that somehow the outer world "knows." But that knowledge is not something our waking mind easily grasps. Apparently here is a meaningful relation among elements of some events which is—what else can we say?—"known"—"but not to our personal consciousness."

Meaning apparently exists apart from our perception of it:

> A "meaning" manifests itself in synchronistic phenomena which appear to be independent of consciousness [199f.]

Is it clear why she says "independent of consciousness"? I didn't intend ahead of time to pick up the letter; the man did not intend ahead of time to find a book about Montalcino. Meaning apparently exists independent of conscious intention.

> This quality of knowledge is what Jung calls "absolute knowledge," since it seems to be detached from our consciousness. In other words, although the initial significance of a synchronistic event can only be experienced subjectively, the fact of a meaningful coincidence on psychic and physical levels suggests that the meaning may also have been originally present in the objective event itself; something rational or similar to *meaning may inhere in the event itself.*[119] [200, emphasis added]

How did we get from an examination of the fact that some dual mandalas are those used for oracular "reads" on time to a consideration of "absolute knowledge"? Von Franz has broached both of these subjects to convey a sense that our grasp of matter is inadequate. There is no Western recognition of meaning in matter:

> In his work on synchronicity, Jung cites a number of other thinkers, both ancient and medieval, who believed in an *oulomelia*, a *correspondentia* or sympathy of all things, whose "meaning" lay hidden in objective phenom-

---

[119] Readers familiar with the life and inner world of Wolfgang Pauli will appreciate this statement: "The idea that meaning lies concealed in events themselves was, as Richard Wilhelm has shown, predominant in earliest Chinese culture." [200f.] No wonder that as Pauli considered the questions we are discussing here he dreamed of Chinese men and women, particularly women. (See van Erkelens, "Wolfgang Pauli and the Chinese *Anima* Figure," pp. 21ff.)

ena of the outer world and could be investigated with the help of mantic procedures. These are the residue of a primitive magical type of thinking which has been more or less eliminated in the development of our more exact modern sciences. In the course of the development of these sciences, however, the baby has, as so often before, been thrown out with the bathwater, so that the directly observable manifestations of "absolute knowledge" in the collective unconscious have also been thrown away. [201]

Okay to Skim

Pages 200-202 we can skim. Von Franz talks about examples of mandalas dealing with memory. I don't think we need to worry about that. They are examples of mandalas dealing with "this earthly side" of the equation. Again, stick with the main idea: how is it that this world can be intelligent? I think we can skip pages 202-203 also. She continues to make the point that intelligence can exist apart from consciousness. Butterflies, for example, exhibit an incredible intelligence in their migratory flight.[120]

On pages 204-205 she discusses divination mandalas, and I have suggested the sense of keeping one example, astrology, in mind as a reference point.[121] My feeling is that the main idea in the chapter is the notion of the intelligence of matter and the challenge to our assumptions about what knowing is that is posed by synchronicity and oracles. Pages 205-

---

[120] The monarch deserves comment: "[For] every fourth or fifth generation of monarch butterflies that summer in the U.S. east of the Continental Divide, the pull of high-altitude Oyamel fir forests in central Mexico is irresistible.

"By the millions each fall they point south and flutter up to 2,000 miles to reach the forests on a few small mountain peaks in an approximately 60-square-mile area in the volcanic highlands that serve as the butterflies' winter retreat.

"For scientists, this annual migration is one of nature's greatest mysteries. Four to five generations separate the monarch populations that make the migration, so the butterflies that make the trek to Mexico are the great, great grandchildren of the previous generation to have made it." (John Roach, "Internal Clock Leads Monarch Butterflies to Mexico")

That is to say, no mama or papa butterfly teaches them to do it. They (insects) find their distant destination expertly while I (human) often get lost driving to the dentist's office just downtown.

[121] For an enlightening meld of astrology and analytical psychology, see Alice O. Howell, *The Heavens Declare: Astrological Ages and the Evolution of Consciousness.*

207 have to do with Descartes discovering the Cartesian coordinate system (graphing formulas that we learned in algebra). The coordinate system is another form of the mandala that deals with concrete space.[122]

Cybernetics

What is cybernetics? It is the discipline that gave birth to the computer. Cybernetics tries to investigate how animals and people process information, and then seeks to build machines that do the same thing. In this last section of the chapter von Franz attempts to build a bridge between the cyberneticist's understanding of information and our understanding of ascertaining the meaning of a moment by recourse to oracular methods, for example, a throw of the I Ching. She refers to the cybernetic use of the word "entropy."

Entropy is a term from thermodynamics that represents the unavailability of energy in a system.[123] That sounds convoluted, but it isn't really. Take a big block of ice. That ice has the capacity to cool the air around it as it melts. The temperature of the ice and the temperature of the air around it will eventually become the same. The ice will become warmer water and the air around will become a little cooler. When the ice and the air are at the same temperature the ice will no longer be able to cool the air. The ice has lost its capacity to cool the air: its entropy has increased. *The law of entropy states that when there is an energy transfer from one object to another, that transfer is irreversible.*

That is to say, the ice can make the air cooler, but all that "coolness" in the air will never flow back and become a block of ice again. Another way to put it is that entropy is a measure of the evenness with which energy (here think temperature) is distributed. At the end of the ice's melting, the temperature of the water and the temperature of the surrounding air will be pretty much the same. There will be no more interaction between them.

Also, when there was a block of ice and warm air, there were two

---

[122] Her footnote reference 29 on page 206 points us to a very interesting discussion of Descartes' discovery from the point of view of his dreams. ("The Dream of Descartes," *Timeless Documents of the Soul*, pp. 65ff. It has also been published in her *Dreams*, pp. 107ff.)

[123] Isaac Asimov, *Understanding Physics: Motion, Sound, and Heat, Vol.1*, pp. 231-240.

parts to the story. There was the block of ice and there was the air. A state of coldness in one part and a state of warmth in the other. This is said to be the "ordered" state of the system. It is like we put our shoes in one corner of the room and our books on the table. Surely over time our shoes will end up strewn over the floor and our books will be flopped among them as we do our homework; so the "coldness" of the ice and the "warmth" of the air will mix, like shoes and books, as the cold ice becomes warm water and the warm air becomes a little cooler. There is an increase in disorder among the ice and water as there was in the room with the shoes and the books. An increase in entropy is also an increase in disorder.

Von Franz then refers to the cybernetic idea that understanding amounts to a reduction of entropy (increase in order):

> At this point, cybernetics introduces still another new idea: every increase of information is equivalent to the possibility of a system's entropic state being reduced by an ordering intervention. [208]

When there is understanding between a subject and a process, the overall order between the two of them is increased, says the cyberneticist. Understanding brings order. For a non-cyberneticist that statement sounds strange. However we are considering it not because of its meaning in cybernetics, but because of its psychological meaning as a metaphor for our own quest toward consciousness. We have already talked about the capacity of consciousness to bring order, that is, meaningful development, into our lives. Von Franz has merely noted that cyberneticists, too, have talked about understanding as bringing order into the system of the understanding subject and an understood process.

But it must be a certain type of understanding which has the capacity to bring order, says the cyberneticist:

> In order to realize the ordering intervention in a system, the observing psyche must, of course, transform its merely passive, contemplative attitude into an active and voluntatively[124] intervening one. The possibility of

---

[124] "Voluntative" means proceeding from the will and desire; *Oxford English Dictionary*, CD-ROM.

counteracting the law of entropy by a law of negentropy which exists in the psyche, not in the sphere of individual consciousness but in what [French physicist Oliver Costa] de Beauregard, viewing it as a cosmic actuality, terms the *infrapsychisme.* [209][125]

Again von Franz sees the parallel between cybernetic reflection on the nature and effect of knowing and our recognition of two dimensions. It is easy to see a connection between de Beauregard's statement of an "infra [=inner]-psychisme" which registers knowing [209], and our understanding of the transcendental continuum as the deeper knowing within ourselves. Realized order, or meaning, is finally not possible as an act of individual consciousness alone; it only possible when there is an interaction with, or a consciousness of, a greater dimension and knowing, access to which entails our undertaking to comprehend the world in front of us and its meaning.

---

[125] I have slightly modified the translation of the second sentence. The German text reads: "Die Möglichkeit, dem Entropiegesetz entgegenzuwirken (Negentropiegesetz) liegt in der Psyche, aber nicht im Individual-Bewußtsein, sondern in etwas, was Costa de Beauregard als "infra-psychisme" bezeichnet hat, worin er eine *kosmische Gegebenheit* sieht." (Von Franz, *Zahl und Zeit*, p.187. *Zahl und Zeit* is the original German version of *Number and Time*)

Chapter 12

The Archetype of the Number-Game as the Basis of Probability Theory and Number Oracles

I was once talking to a physician and I told him how Jungian analysis can in fact have an effect on the body. I related the situation of a fellow I worked with analytically whose diabetes went into remission during the course of our work, at least for a couple of years. It eventually returned, but he was spared many months of suffering.

My analysand and I had interpreted his diabetes from the symbolic point of view, and I promise you it made a difference. So I explained this to the medical doctor, saying, "And that is data." He replied, "No, it's not. That's not data, it's an anecdote."

Why was it not data? Because it was not repeatable. The scientific paradigm considers real only what is repeatable, what can be shown to happen over and over again, given an identical setup and identical procedure. But the problem of this way of looking at things is that there was only one of that man, my analysand. For the scientific method, something is "true" only insofar as it corresponds to an average among a number of instances. However, in analytical psychology every instance we work with is a unique one. Therefore our stance is negated by the traditional scientific mentality.

Don't just think of the scientific mentality as something "out there." It permeates everything we do. If we have been able to cut through the contemporary fashion of cynicism within ourselves, it will have become clear how the fascination with large numbers infects everyone.[126]

Spirit Lost

Von Franz begins this chapter with a discussion of spirit, and with the observation that numbers are one of the psyche's prime ways of expressing that spirit. This we have already touched on in chapters 3 and 8 and need not repeat. Then on page 214 she cites qualities of the spirit being

---

[126] Remember "studies showed . . ."? We are acculturated to this scientific paradigm.

"active, winged, animating, stimulating, inspiring," meaning that these are the effects on our emotional well-being of following the direction in life that is charted out for us by the inner guidance of (sequentially evolving) dreams and synchronicities.

As we have been saying, this ordering factor is a "non-ego" capacity, something that emerges spontaneously from the inside (and outside in synchronicities), not something we consciously think up and plan. But in modern times our ability to create life from spontaneous inner guidance has more and more been understood as something the conscious ego can do solely on its own resources, as an act of will. There is an increasing emphasis in the West on our determining the course of our lives solely by deliberate choice rather than by an inquiry into our greater pattern, as manifested, for example, in dreams. It is, of course, possible simply to determine the course of our life by willpower, but the results are much more paltry. Dreams and a disciplined imagination, as portals for the spirit, have a much greater scope when it comes to distinguishing what we are capable of and how to form that into reality. They are the way to make and keep life juicy.

But:

> The history of the development of mathematics demonstrates this gradual "subjectification" of the spirit particularly clearly. [215]

The modern mind thinks it can create the pattern which makes life meaningful; it is hardly interested in "reading" the images that can guide us toward an authentic life. Just go to a bookstore and compare the number of books dealing with dreams against the number of those dealing with the habits of highly whatever people. Parallel with fast lanes and trendy McMansions is a faith in large numbers that does not admit the qualitative value of the single number, the single small instance, the unique individual. Thus von Franz writes:

> Whereas the Pythagoreans considered numbers to be spiritual/material cosmic principles, and even Leopold Kronecker [a nineteenth-century German mathematician[127] who said "The integers were created by God;

---

[127] "Leopold Kronecker," Wikipedia.

all else is man-made."] continued to ascribe their origins to a creative act of God, they are now viewed to be pure "constructions" of human consciousness by many contemporary mathematicians. They are evaluated as the signs with which consciousness "plays," according to specific rules laid down by itself. [215 and note].

The point of view that sees numbers as quantities and ignores that numbers are also symbols of individual value is another form of our tendency to treat ourselves, and others, as numbers (meaning valueless quantities) and not as personalities. Therein lies the foundation of an impersonal, perhaps fascistic, society.

Statistics

Von Franz continues:

A parallel development may also be observed in modern physics, as it makes increasing use of the probability concept, which ignores all exceptional unique facts as much as possible. [216]

The danger is that this aspect of the scientific worldview becomes our guiding metaphor. To my feeling, the emotional significance of quantum physics' discovery concerning the unpredictability of electrons is to remind us to be open to the nonpredictability and meaning of single events. But in fact the *method* of science is to disregard that and only consider real what is ascertained when the unpredictable element is excluded. So the issue in quantum research has been to investigate the *average* movements of electrons as they produce predictable bands of light from energized molecules. It is true there is no way to know the movement of a single electron, but along with that limitation comes the tendency to define individual events as "anecdotes" not worthy of recognition.

She continues:

The greatest possible repetition of experiments reflects an effort on the part of man to forcibly channel events within the scope of probability theory, because the latter can only attain precision through the greatest possible number of repetitions. Only under this condition do significant trends become observable. Modern scientific experimentation is built up entirely on this assumption that only very extensive repetition of experiments yields significant results. This [reflects the] modern scientific faith in the "law of large numbers." [216]

The irony is that, historically speaking, numbers in human consciousness were first images of the spirit—witness the Pythagoreans—but the way they are often understood by the traditional scientific mind negates their original meaning. The "law of large numbers" holds a dangerous sway:

> The extent to which statistics, in its applied and dogmatic form, has become a destructive, deadly tool in the hands of sociologists and politicians today need not be emphasized. [218]

That is just one aspect of number.

Spirit Found

> When today we believe we have uncovered nature's secrets through probability theory or statistics, we too have fallen victim to an inflation . . . . For "faith in large numbers" causes an inflated identification of consciousness with what is merely one aspect of . . . number, set up in opposition to unique events. [219f.]

Number as the tool for computing averages—and who among us does not judge ourselves against a real or imagined average?—is only one half of the story. The other aspect of number, number in its original sense of symbol, conveys the ability to look at single events and persons from the point of view of their intrinsic value, not from the point of view of where they fit into the average. Number, it is worth repeating, is originally a reflection of the spirit that produces an individual. But to the extent that we are living a "numerically quantitative" life, we will honor the more "average," over and against the creative value of the individual citizen.

I was talking to a woman recently who was going though a difficult situation and she just spontaneously associated to a number dream, "I simply feel like I don't count." It is when we look at life with the hidden quantitative assumptions of "large numbers"—and have lost feeling for the qualitative individuality expressed, for example, by the Pythagoreans view of numbers as sacred—that we feel we don't count.

These two views of number are then summed up by von Franz:

> The opposition of "scientific experiment" and "oracle of divination" in modern thought has led to a split in the paradoxical dual nature of the number archetype. In experiments, an effort is made, by repetition, to thrust aside number's individual aspect under the heading of "chance." In oracles, on the other hand, chance is accorded a central position. [220]

In the throw of an oracle such as the I Ching, we create a chance event. In a scientific experiment we seek to get rid of the chance event. But chance is the way the deeper order of a life appears. The I Ching—or a synchronicity—is a chance event with a message. It is through these "voices" that the direction intended by the spirit can be known. By recognizing the fallacy of "faith in large numbers" and by holding on to the value of the single number, the single event, the qualitatively individual, the spirit—as the future-creating capacity of nature—has the possibility of realizing its goal, and thus we have the opportunity of fulfilling our deepest purpose.

Oracles and Chance

Von Franz examines the oracular understanding of number, and refers to the scientific sanctity of the repeatable event:

> What differentiates probability theory in quantum physics (and experiments coordinated with it) from that in "oracles" is the frequent repetition of "throws" [meaning the experiments], in order to reduce the factor of chance to a minimum. In divinatory oracles (the I Ching, for instance), on the other hand, single chance throws become *the* center of attention and form the starting point for all deliberations. Experiments are repeated frequently in time and serve to fix an isolated sector of the universe, while oracles occur only once. [222]

> How then is it possible that oracular techniques exist based on repeated "throws" in time? And how is it that the Chinese tried to predict synchronistic phenomena when, by definition, these are creative acts? Clearly a certain "probability" also exists in the psychological realm; it is based on the collective substratum of the individual psyche, on archetypal structural dispositions which remain largely unchanged in the depths reaching beyond all personal variations. [223]

I'd like to linger on this phrase: "archetypal structural dispositions." That is to say, we are trying to read an activated archetype in throwing the I Ching. The I Ching echoes the potential in a given situation, and that potential comes from the fact that an archetype is activated and is seeking expression. Recall that archetypes are not limited simply to the psyche; so when an archetype is activated it has both a material and a psychic aspect: it has an effect both in the psyche and at times in the physical world. The I Ching likewise transverses two domains of experience—our meaning, the situation in outer reality—and the relation between the two.

> Whereas the precision of probability theory in the quantitative realm is increased through repetition, psychological probability theory must draw archetypal situations into the center of observation, as most oracular and divinatory techniques do. [223f.]

Where science looks for the average, we seek the singular event which is a way to "read" the archetype that is constellated ... as it is affecting the single, emotional individual in this single moment of time. No "faith in large numbers" here.

One more comment on chance is called for:

> In experimentation the observer's conscious ego cuts a particular system out of the realm of wholeness. [The experimenter does his or her best to get rid of chance, though this chance, too, is part of life.] But in the oracle one allows chance to make the cut and only subsequently tries to read the result from it [we try to give chance its voice]. [224]

Get Excited

Von Franz continues the discussion of chance and probability through page 227. Then she looks at the emotional significance of the chance theme. She first mentions it on pages 224f.:

> "Dynamically excited" *unconscious* contents seem to be bound up with the appearance of synchronistic events. *Logically they invalidate the law of (meaningless) chance.*

And then she returns to the same on page 227:

> This setup can only lead to results if an archetype and its accompanying

high charge of psychic energy are already constellated in the unconscious. For this reason, all divinatory techniques operate with the warning they are only to be used in "serious situations," and the question is never to be repeated in a spirit of frivolity. The greater the psychic tension the more probable and to the point the result.

Both synchronistic events and the effectiveness of oracular questioning seem to be dependent on our being able to carry the tension of the unknown. So when suffering over an issue, the most important quality we can bring to the situation is the ability to hold our question alive, to feel the emotional weight it brings, not to leap into action but to continue to feel what we are feeling despite the unpleasantness or misery that we are probably experiencing. Then the unconscious can respond with a dream, a synchronistic event, or an oracular read on the meaning of the situation that is not trivial, that echoes in its accuracy the seriousness with which we are approaching this, and each, step in life.

Creative Personalities

Von Franz ends this chapter with further reflections on chance:

> Whatever cannot be consciously systematized nowadays is termed "chance," with the implication that it is not worthy of further investigation. But it is just in such "chance" occurrences that startling new ideas erupt. It is being more and more firmly established that parapsychological phenomena occur mainly in the surroundings of an individual *whom the unconscious wants to take a step in the development of consciousness*, as, for instance, adolescents who must take the "leap" into adulthood. Creative personalities who must fulfill a new creative task intended by the unconscious also attract such phenomena . . . . This means that whenever a creative intention is present in the unconscious, parapsychological and particularly synchronistic phenomena, which Jung calls "acts of creation," may be expected. Oracular techniques of the past actually represented efforts to grasp, by means of games of chance, the general psychological quality of the content constellated in the unconscious. [230f.]

It turns out that anecdotes signal the most important moments of all.

PART V

Number and the Parapsychological Aspects of the Principle of Synchronicity

Chapter 13

Number, Time, and Synchronicity

The essence of chapter 13 can be expressed in one word: *kairos*. This was what the Greeks in antiquity understood as the qualitative aspect of time. For them *chronos* (as in chronometer) designated time as duration; *kairos*, time as *quality*. If time were a yardstick, chronos would be the space between the ticks of the yardstick clock and *kairos* would be the quality of the space between the ticks.

Not all moments have the same *kairos*. Where the space between the ticks is always identical, the quality of what happens there need not be. Von Franz contends that not only does time possess a *qualitative* distinction, but also the nature of these special moments is to recur rhythmically.

Number as Motion in Time

She begins the chapter with the notion that number represents

> *a psychophysical motion-pattern . . . intimately connected with the problem of time.* [235]

Numbers represent a dynamism which moves life forward by its symbolic appearance in both dreams as images and in the material world as synchronicity. The spirit, in other words, is an active "force" with an inner intelligence that solicits our psychological maturation by continually creating suggestions for our next step in development, the next insights we are to integrate, the next values we are to adopt, the next phases of our involvement. The job of the spirit is forward change in our personal development. And when the time is ripe for us to take these steps, the images that will guide us appear inwardly and outwardly. So growth, and the right time for growth, we know belong together.

She continues explicating this position through page 242, emphasizing the cyclic character of the time moment. Here is an example:

> In other words, the extraworldly timeless order of the "Earlier Heaven" is transformed into a temporal one (time being regarded cyclically in China) and is thereby specifically altered. [239]

The "Earlier Heaven" in the Chinese expression would equate to what we have called the transcendental continuum. It is the given pattern of our life. That is presented to us step-by-step as the dynamism we have called spirit parses successive pieces of our life to us in the appropriate moment of time. If we can grasp what is being presented to us we have the possibility of altering our lives. Also we find in the Chinese understanding she refers to an awareness that there is a cyclic character to these potentially life-altering "appropriate moments." This she will examine more closely.

She then acquaints us with an ancient Chinese shamanistic divinatory technique of spinning in opposite directions two small boards which rotated around a center post. A numerical sketch representing the heavenly pattern was drawn on one board; a numerical outline representing life on earth in time was drawn on the other. When the two boards came to a rest the numerical relation between them was read to portray the character of a given moment:

> The unification of the two arrangements signifies the coming together of an eternal order . . . with the just-so-ness of reality. [241f.]

The eternal character of the eternal world of possibility was thought to

> break into ordinary time, appearing to individuals as meaningful arrangements of inner and outer factors. [243]

She has just elucidated the Chinese understanding of the relation of the eternal world of possibility to the time-bound nature of reality through an example of divination from ancient China. Her point was to observe not only how Asian antiquity conceived of the two dimensions of life and time, but also to show that it acknowledged a rhythmic understanding of the two dimensions. Where the shaman could *repeatedly* construct a bridge between an earthly moment and its meaning, so in our idiom would synchronicity repeatedly bring the transcendental message into time.

Acausal Orderedness

The "acausal orderedness" she refers to with respect to the "heavenly" side of the shaman's divinatory tool (and the transcendental continuum in general) is one of Jung's far-reaching concepts. Whereas the basic assumptions of biology, take evolution for example, are that natural processes are random and only achieve the forms of life by trial and error, Jung sees in the "natural" processes of synchronicity the attempts of nature to pattern and develop herself. There is no recognizable "cause" for this; it just happens. He is suggesting that there is an organizing principle to life within life itself.

For the life of an individual this unquestionably means that the choices of the will are not the only way we grow. We are patterned to grow emotionally by a sort of "inner reason" that is not a conscious act, though consciousness must certainly cooperate with the hints that are dropped into dreams and meaningful events. Naturally as a psychiatrist Jung was most interested in the role of "acausal orderedness" in the psychological development of individuals. But in the years since Jung's death other scientists have seen, and are exploring, this orderedness in a whole range of other contexts. Within what is today called "complexity theory" we can, in effect, observe Jung's recognition of this strange kind of ordering. A full consideration of that research is outside the scope of this introduction to *Number and Time*, but I felt it worthwhile to note how Jung introduced a concept fifty years ago that is now finding greater independent currency, even outside of psychology.[128]

---

[128] See Melanie Mitchell, *Complexity: A Guided Tour*. She observes: "Nigel Franks, a biologist specializing in ant behavior, has written, 'If 100 army ants are placed on a flat surface, they will walk around . . . until they die of exhaustion.' Yet put a half a million

Von Franz then cites some very interesting dreams that Jung felt portrayed just this acausal orderedness:

> In his paper on synchronicity Jung himself relates several dreams which allude to this phenomenon: in one of them the woman dreamer finds layers of rock with black squares on them, so exactly formed as to give the impression of being drawn by a human hand. [246]

It is as if nature somehow has a human imprint. Or we could say the events in a synchronicity are that human imprint in nature being shown to us—something which is both in us and in the material world.

> In [another dream] a man likewise comes across a rock face with a low relief with human heads on it and rock pillars with capitals of carved human heads. They are also found in places where they could not have been created by human hands. [246]

Those dreams express a very similar idea. There is this human imprint in nature, which would be, in our way of conceiving it, an archetypal form also in the material world.

> The dreams describe . . . the meaningful coincidence of an absolutely natural product with a human idea . . . apparently independent of it. [246]

Von Franz then mentions another dream, described by Jung, with a similar import. It is the ending of the dream that I find so telling:

> The next moment each of these chance forms had vanished without trace.[129] [246]

That is to say, the ordering factor appears at only certain moments. She then continues her discussion, and those further examples convey her overall idea.

---

of them together, and the group as a whole becomes what some have called a 'superorganism' with 'collective intelligence.'" (p. 3) For example they can build bridges "with their bodies to allow the colony to take the shortest path across a gap." (p. 5) While causality assumes the whole is the sum of its parts, there clearly are situations where the whole is *more* than the sum of its parts. Where does that new order or intelligence come from? It is not causally explicable. It is "acausally" organized.

[129] "Synchronicity," *The Structure and Dynamics of the Psyche,* CW 8, pars. 945f.

It's About Time

Von Franz then returns to the question of *kairos* and rhythm:

> Until recently, time was almost exclusively analyzed in terms of spatial analogies. [249]

There are two errors in the visualization of time as the space between the ticks of a clock. First, that picture ignores the *quality* of time between the ticks; it dismisses the idea that there are qualitatively different moments in life. And, second, it conceives of time as linear—the yardstick. But time is not merely a straight line; it is also cyclic, rhythmic. A synchronistic moment is a "return" to the oneness of our complete potential.

In a synchronicity the transcendental continuum "drops down" and conveys a little chunk of our real self, the real values and opportunities that are there for us to make part of our life and the community around us. So these special moments are "return" moments in which we get a partial glimpse of the whole, and in that sense they are a reappearance of the genuine whole, albeit in a single attribute, pertinent to the "right moment" of their manifestation.

Hence she wants to consider the assertion that:

> *the universe possesses one single fundamental rhythm,* on which our whole concept of physical time might possibly have to be based. . . . *Time is based on rhythms, instead of rhythms being based on time.* [250f.]

Putting it similarly she observes that we normally think of time as "a linear sequence of clearly differentiable acts," [252] whereas it is more likely that time is "the fundamental rhythm of the number series." [252]

Her points are not as abstract as they might sound. Our common understanding of time is that it goes on and on. Take the state of despair, for example. If we have been through the valley of the shadow of death, in those states of mind it seems that the darkness will never end. It seems that it will go on continually, in a never-changing straight line, forever. Or if we are on a high of success, we may forget to be careful as we act like the good times will last forever. But the real nature of life is a mixture of dark and light. And the fact is that periods end. A return to possibility and hopefulness inevitably follows if we face the dark periods consciously, watching our dreams, querying the meaning of the emptiness and loss of hope. Contrariwise, successes easily go sour. In fact time's pendulum swings back again from defeat and we are once more put in touch with our source: what comes is a new inspiration from within, a new possibility from the outside, a new friendship which can receive what has been generating within during the period of felt loss. Likewise gifts can easily evaporate if carelessly attended to out of the shortsightedness of elation. Time does cycle back to different qualitative moments, though our normative grasp of it is that it is linear and unchanging. We forget that within time are "possible future states." [253]

Acts of Creation

To say that time is rhythmic or cyclic is to say that it is creative. In its return, new possibilities emerge:

> The manifestation of an archetype in synchronistic phenomena can appear both as an "act of creation in time" and as the "eternal presence of this single act." [254]

The "eternal presence of this single act" is a reference to the dynamic tendency to realization within the transcendental continuum. This creative force is a constant given within us, within life as well it seems. Synchronicities are not merely lucky discrete events which confront us occasionally; they are a "piece" of an ever-present creative principle in life that manifests now and then. That creative force is "eternal" and it manifests in time.

Now here is a mouthful:

> Just as the quantitative aspect of the number series is isomorphic with a causal linear time sequence, so too the qualitative aspect of number, because of its retrograde connection to the one-continuum, produces an isomorphism with the timeless primal unity of existence and its synchronistic manifestations. [254]

Let's look at that. Isomorphic means "the same shape as" or "an analogous shape to." Here she is returning to the notion that if we look at numbers as quantities, then they are what mark out the space between the ticks. *One* second, *two* seconds, *three* seconds, etc. But if we look at numbers as qualities, then time is something else. Then numbers are the manifestation of a pattern of wholeness which is preexistent to us, and the expression of that pattern in time is a synchronicity. Synchronicity harkens back to the source of our potential and brings a piece of it forward in image form into the present moment. When the "time is ripe." [255]

To conclude her consideration of the creative nature of time, from pages 256-259 she surveys several deities who both represent time and also are the creators of the world or the generative power of the universe. They are mythological images of what she has wanted to convey by "acts of creation in time."

The *fenestra aeternitatis*

The last point in this chapter is the idea of the *fenestra aeternitatis*, the window on eternity. Look at figure 17 and the picture will convey more than I can explain. A synchronicity is a glimpse. In a synchronistic moment we glimpse into another dimension of life. And at the same time we see the unity of the spiritual and the material. It occurs in a moment of time, but we have to peek our heads into the source of the transcendental, into dreams as the mouthpiece of genuine possibility, to nudge it along. When we make that effort to be true both to the demands of the earth and also to our own given, genuine possible selfhood, a sort of interlocking of the two realms can occur:

> The mysterious point of contact between the two systems appears to be the center or a sort of pivot where psyche and matter meet. [263]

And:

> When such a constellation exists and eternity breaks through momentarily into our temporal system, the primal unity actively manifests itself and temporarily unites the double structures into one. [263]

If we are willing to stick out our neck.

Figure 17. The Hole Open to Eternity; nineteenth-century woodcut.

Chapter 14

The *Unus Mundus* as the World of the Spirit and "Spirits"

Von Franz returns here to the spirit, that "breathlike presence." [265] We experience it in our dream images as they unfold into a story that leads us step-by-step through our genuine, authentic life. In this chapter she investigates images of "spirits," spirits of the dead, that is, ghosts, as another possible metaphor for grasping the nature of spirit. "Spirits," then, in the way they appear in myth and dream, may be able to show us characteristics of the "breathlike presence." She will offer a psychological interpretation of spirits.[130]

Fa and Gba'adu

She studies myths about the land of the dead from the point of view of several cultures: the Fon tribe of West Africa, medieval alchemy, ancient Egypt, and ancient China. I am going to restrict my commentary here to the West African Fon tribe,[131] because one example will be representative for the chapter.

---

[130] That is not to say that dreams and experiences of ghosts are all merely psychological, but that in examining their appearances, particularly in myth, we can learn something about how the spirit works.

It is interesting to see how Jung put the psychology of spirits. The following is a quote from his 1919 essay, "The Psychological Foundation of the Belief in Spirits." "Parapsychic phenomena . . . are, so far as my experience goes, the exteriorized effects of unconscious complexes. I for one am certainly convinced that they are exteriorizations [of psychological complexes]. I have repeatedly observed the telepathic effects of unconscious complexes . . . . But in all this I see no proof whatever of the existence of real spirits, and until such proof is forthcoming I must regard this whole territory as an appendix of psychology."

That was 1919. In 1948 he wrote in a footnote to the later edition of this essay: "After collecting psychological experiences from many people and from many countries for fifty years, I no longer feel as certain as I did in 1919, when I wrote this sentence. To put it bluntly, I doubt whether an exclusively psychological approach can do justice to the phenomena in question." In *The Structure and Dynamics of the Psyche*, CW 8, par. 600 & n.

[131] There are about two million Fon living today, largely in Benin, a small country immediately to the west of Nigeria. ("The Fon People"; and "Benin," Wikipedia).

The Fon tribe of West Africa honors a couple of related divinities. One is Fa and the other is Gba'adu. Von Franz recognizes dimensions of the Self in a metaphorical understanding of both these divinities.

Fa represents the knowledge of the greater life. He knows the significance of what each person has the capacity to achieve, and at the same time he has the good will to help people accomplish it. He comes from the land of the dead—that is how he fits into this chapter on spirits—and transmits their tidings. Every person possesses an invisible soul but does not understand the meaning of his or her soul. Fa has the ability to communicate this meaning:

> Fa imparts purely individual information to every person, ignoring the laws and judgments of mankind; only he who obtains information from him in the oracle[132] can really understand to what it relates. He is *not* a force of nature, but rather portrays God's solicitude for his creation. [267]

She then observes that:

> Psychologically Fa represents a symbol of the Self and of "absolute knowledge" . . . [,] an aspect of the Self activating and sustaining the development of higher consciousness in the individual. [268]

Fa then stands for the knowledge that, through the trials and tribulations of daily life, there is the possibility of living meaningfully and of becoming our true selves. In the manner I have previously discussed, as an image of spirit Fa symbolizes the ability to receive our development at the hands of the "breathlike presence" in terms of the images it creates in dreams and in meaningful coincidences.

Additionally there is Gba'adu. He is connected to the other side of life, the destructiveness of drives, chaos, and dangerous passions:

> Gba'adu is greedy for blood; he dispenses life and takes it back. [269]

Now comes a statement that is confusing, but we will make sense of it:

---

[132] She has referred to geomancy with respect to Fa. Geomancy "is a method of divination that interprets markings on the ground or the patterns formed by tossed handfuls of soil, rocks, or sand." ("Geomancy," Wikipedia) Fa brought the art of geomancy from the land of the dead.

"Gba'adu is the most dreaded voodoo, for he possesses the most profound knowledge of Fa." To some extent he portrays a still more comprehensive symbol of the *unus mundus* than Fa, since he embraces all of existence, including its dark, deadly, and chaotic forces. ... Gba'adu, as the mystery beyond earthly existence, cannot be experienced in this life, but is only revealed in death. [269]

That may sound confusing because we have been discussing the *unus mundus* in terms of the unity of existence, the *a priori* [prior to experience, that is, there at birth] plan of our life, etc. Within our discussion, however, has been the tacit assumption that that plan is all hunky dory. But part of our life is meant to include difficulties, setbacks and even tragedy. Of course, we try to do all we can do in analytic work to make life fulfilling and meaningful. In the language of the Fon, that would be to ask "Fa" to help us see the thread of development within the chaos of life's difficult moments. Think of the woman's dreadful experiences with her car; they were very painful, even dangerous, moments in her life, though their symbolic message could be seen as helpful in the long run. They were saying watch out for inner attitudes and outer people who will try to derail you from your goal. Sometimes we have to go through difficult and horrific phases in order to arrive where we are meant to be. Then analytic wisdom consists not in just "making everything great," but in learning how to endure, and be enriched by, life's darkness when it is an essential part of our journey [Gba'adu] with a meaning to be gleaned [Fa].

The cliché of making lemonade from lemons does somewhat fit here, but sometimes a lot of lemons have to be swallowed and many lemon lessons learned before it is time to make the lemonade. And we don't "make" the lemonade, but find it hidden within the lemons themselves. Then we can put forth the effort to find the container from which the lemonade can be poured and shared with others. This ambiguity of suffering and growth is more clearly expressed in Gba'adu than in Fa; that is why von Franz refers to Gba'adu as an apt representation of the *unus mundus*. Fa is strength to inquire into, and the knowing about, life's "Gba'adu" aspect—intended though both chaos and meaning may be—so that we may fulfill ourselves through good and ill.

The lesson to be gleaned from Fa and Gba'adu is that other cultures have distinguished between the meaning of life (the potential of genuine selfhood within the transcendental continuum which the spirit tries to communicate) and the events of life in time and space which may or may not be felicitous but may contain guidance about our legitimate path.

Life Deposit

We have looked at one of the examples from several mythological traditions that von Franz cites to link up the land of the dead and the transcendental continuum or greater pattern. The idea, similar to what we have been otherwise portraying, is that the world of potential selfhood exists in another "dimension" apart from time and space.

We don't know what that other dimension definitely is but we do infer its existence from the order of life that can be seen hidden in some of its events. The land of the dead is an added way that the other dimension has been formulated in not a few mythologies. It struck von Franz as extremely curious that the land of the dead should be described as the place where the knowledge of life's meaning was hidden. The implication remains that there is some sort of knowing attributed to the spirit world, the land of the dead. How did it get there? Again, thinking in an "as if" way, she puts forward the idea, also found in mythological traditions, that somehow life leaves a deposit "there," in the realm apart from daily living:

> According to the main argument of this book, it appears that matter and psyche form merely the inner and the outer aspects of the same transcendental reality. We ventured this conclusion because the ultimate constituents of matter present themselves to our observing consciousness in forms similar to those forms representing the ultimate foundations of the inner factor, the collective unconscious. This transcendental unitary reality (*unus mundus*) calls forth the hypothesis of animate matter. We know that at death the material part of a man dissolves into inorganic material constituents, into something, therefore, which modern physics would define as an electromagnetic field, whose excited points represent particles. The old religious texts referred to, which aim, as it were, at an introspective per-

ception of the same process, describe death as an ascension into the realm of the gods, i.e., into the archetypal field of the collective unconscious. [278]

Von Franz finds that assertion a little more fully registered in the early Chinese mind:

> The Chinese concept of life after death, as described by Richard Wilhelm, seems to me to throw interesting light on this problem. The Chinese distinguish between a bodily and a psychic aspect of man, which both disperse at death into an animated universal substance. But a psychic element survives as a third factor capable of consciousness; it consists of a tendency to consciousness, so to speak, which must, however, be concentrated during the course of one's lifetime so as to survive death. [279]

I'll give a dream example.

A man in his thirties was contemplating suicide, and he discussed with me his loss of belief in the value of life. During this time he dreamed that he had committed suicide and had gone to his own funeral. It dawned on him in the dream to wonder how he could both be dead and at the same time at his funeral with consciousness of the event. He saw himself lying in the casket. He saw the people gathered around it, and so on. Then he realized that at death consciousness is not extinguished, it continues. That is how he could both be dead as well as watching what was going on. He also realized from his unhappy feeling in the dream that the level of consciousness we take to eternity is the level of consciousness of our anima or animus which we have achieved before death. So if our anima or animus is fulfilled when we die, that state of mind is what lives on in the afterlife, forever.

For a man, of course, it would be the level of consciousness of the anima, for a woman the level of consciousness of the animus. The body dies but the state of the anima or animus achieved in life is what lives on in the state of mind after death. The dreamer next realized to his horror that his suicide hadn't made any difference; it hadn't made anything any better. That was bad news! There he was at his funeral feeling miserable (the misery of his anima before death), and that misery would never change. What he was feeling in his life, in other words the state of his anima, was now his state of mind forever. That would go on; he hadn't solved anything by shooting himself. The desolation would continue. The only thing that was altered by suicide was that in death he had lost his ability to change his despair into fulfillment. Death removed the possibility of choice. What a shock that gave him! He realized that suicide was no way out. Well, the man didn't kill himself.

I see in the man's dream an illustration of what the texts von Franz refers to are expressing. The text she cites calls it a substance. That might be a good way of visualizing it. Whatever it is, there is a decent possibility something is concentrated somewhere during the course of our lifetime. Something is accrued. The text calls it a substance; the man's dream called it the state of the anima or animus, accrued through hard effort. That is what survives death.

Von Franz—and I—have entertained these thoughts as another way to conceptualize that there is something beyond the particulars of daily living in which some sort of pattern for, and value of, life can be inferred to exist. Full living involves the concerted effort of constant inquiry into what lies beyond, or beneath, the appearances of everyday experience and the constant devotion to the enterprise of making that real here, concretely, in the way we conduct our lives.

Chapter 15

Synchronicity and the *Coniunctio*

Impersonal and Personal Eros

A summary of the chapter is on page 292:

> *In a synchronistic event a coniunctio of two cosmic principles*, namely, *of psyche and matter, takes place*, and in the process a real "exchange of attributes" occurs as well. In such situations the psyche behaves as if it were material and matter behaves as if it belonged to the psyche.

A synchronicity is a union of the material world and the spiritual world. Uniting is the business of Eros. Synchronicity, then, is a type of Eros. Eros is more than what happens between two people. Perhaps I could say that there is a personal and an impersonal Eros. The personal Eros is what draws two people together into a union; impersonal Eros is the union of the two parts of life that we normally consider separate: inside and outside, spirit and matter. Hence von Franz writes:

> Number makes its appearance in this context as the *vinculum amoris*, the bond of love which unites the two principles by jointly ordering them. [292]

That is the impersonal Eros aspect of a synchronicity.

Then she makes an elegant comment about personal Eros:

> A preconscious spiritual order lies at the base of all love relationships. Because there seems to exist such a spiritual "objective" order at the base of Eros, it is expressed in the seemingly abstract, feelingless, impersonal order of numbers, as a clear, immutable factor free from illusions. [293]

Not only is there an objective patterning in the impersonal Eros of synchronicity, but personal Eros, the love between two people, is based on this objective dimension. In other words, two people are meant for each other. That would be a more prosaic way of putting it. It is not that desire and love simply bring people together. It is like there are two destinies that belong together; desire and love, then, are the means whereby their belonging together is brought about.

164

This cosmic ordering of the Self constitutes the ultimate mystery behind all human desire and behavior, an unfathomable and fearsome mystery. [293]

On the personal level this is what is ultimately at stake when two people are really brought into connection in love. The question of destiny is what lends love and desire their overwhelming power.

Both in the union of synchronicity and in the personal union of two lovers is to be found "this inexorable objective order behind all existence." [293]

Tepëu and Cucumáz

Von Franz instances several examples in which there is an association between number, love, and fate. She refers to a Buddhist story about marriage, a Mayan oracle, the West Nigerian geomancy I looked at in the last chapter, an ancient Egyptian text, an alchemical text, and ancient pictures in Chinese tombs. I would like to mention one of these, the Mayan *tzité* oracle.

In that oracle *tzité* beans and kernels of corn were thrown.

> The grains of corn stood for the feminine element . . . . the *tzité* beans for the masculine. [286]

The message of the oracle was read by the way they landed on the ground. The intermingling of the beans and the corn was thought to be a sexual union between the world creators Tepëu and Cucumáz:

> The *coniunctio* significance of this oracle can be traced back to the Mayan creation myth on the makings of man, preserved in the Quiche Mayan Book of Counsel. [286]

She then cites the myth which I include here in part:

> In darkness and night Tepëu and Cucumáz came together and spoke with each other ... And they perceived that with the light, man must appear. In this fashion they agreed upon Creation. [287]

The throw of the beans and corns represent a union of male and female, "Lie one upon the other! Speak, that we may hear." [287] From this union an oracular response was created, and that union was the echo of the creation of the world at the beginning of the universe as the divinities Tepëu and Cucumáz spoke with each other. Thus the convergence of the timeless plan and the particular requirements of the present moment that we have seen both in oracles and in synchronicity is made complete. That converge is conceived as a sexual union of love.

Love Wounds

There is a practical implication to the fact that synchronicity, the union of inside and outside, matter and spirit, is a kind of Eros. Where we have been hardened to personal love, we will also be closed to the meaning of the impersonal love of synchronicity. Life is continually giving us the right new opportunities to heal and to move forward into meaningful situations where the past does not have to repeat. That is a very simple way of expressing the love or healing power of synchronicity.

Think of my letter and the man's book; both were opportunities and encouragements for us to continue moving forward in our lives to new accomplishments and connections with others. But if we have been hardened to personal love, we will take the same attitude to the benevolence of synchronicity. When there is an attitude, "You don't expect me to trust anybody, do you?" there will be a rejecting attitude toward really coming to grips with what von Franz has been discussing in the book. The response will be, "All this Jungian synchronicity talk is just a bunch of flaky stuff; you don't take it seriously, do you?"

These experiences belong to the heart. If we have been hurt by love, we have to learn both to let another human being touch our hearts and to let events, that is, meaningful coincidences, move us as well. Synchronicities have not only to be experienced in the head, they have to be experienced in the heart. They are prodding us once again to take a chance and open ourselves to belief and risk. Opening ourselves to the timeless is like opening to a lover.[133] To be closed to human warmth is to be

---

[133] Hence St. John of the Cross's "Concerning the Divine Word:" "With the divinest Word, the Virgin | Made pregnant, down the road | Comes walking, if you'll grant her | A room in your abode." *(Poems of St. John of the Cross*, p. 89)

closed to meaning, and to be closed to meaning is to be closed to human warmth. Life is constantly offering second chances, though, of course, never with a guarantee. We have to take the risk of response. For this the heart must be open.

The Deepest Longing

Number and Time ends with a reference to cosmic (that is, impersonal) Eros [299]. In a subtle way von Franz's work all along has been about a love union.

Shortly before I began writing this book I dreamed that a solitary Native American woman in indigenous dress was praying to the father God for his spirit to descend to earth and mingle with the affairs of humans. The prayer comes from the natural American soul long banished by conquest and concrete. Her appeal is for life on earth to be united with its larger plan. But what, in the twenty-first century, is left of her original vision of union? Very little. With the strains of technological routines habitually reducing personal Eros to a shade of its first dignity, the experience of cosmic, impersonal Eros which can move us in a synchronistic occurrence is even more remote. Still Jung's work, regardless of fashion, and always with an eye to the inner source of dreams, returns to beginning visions and sustaining values.

Jung was no stranger to dark valleys of human experience—as is the case with anyone living fully and creatively. But, as he knew, in those valleys were diamonds seeking to enhance life. It was *his* great love that consistently presented them to our time, jewels of understanding desperately needed in an un-jeweled age. Through his psychological inquiry he showed us more of the love union not only between people, but also between people and this something bigger we have been recognizing in the study of Marie-Louise von Franz's remarkable opus.

The native woman's prayer for the spirit to unite with earthly affairs calls for our response to the pattern of heaven in material events. As the spirit descends and we are open to the guidance of its earthly voice, her longing will be answered by the diamonds of our conscious, creative, and meaningful lives.

Summary and Outlook

Page 301

"The concept of natural numbers rests on an archetypal foundation. It represents a preconscious pattern of thought common to all human psyches." [Chapter 8]

"Those aspects of the number archetype which present-day Western mathematics has made conscious in no way exhaust *all* its aspects. In particular, the relation of number to time remains largely unexplained." [Chapter 13]

"The preconscious aspect of natural numbers points to the idea of a numerical *field* in which individual numbers figure as energic phenomena or rhythmic configurations." [Chapter 9]

"This 'field,' [Chapter 8] . . . is organized around the central archetype of the Self." [Chapters 4-7]

"Historical mandala structures deserve particular attention." [Chapters 10-11]

Page 302

"Time does not form an 'empty' frame for the events taking place within it, but rather represents a sequence of qualitative, inescapable conditions for the events possible at any given moment." [Chapter 13]

"This orderly sequence is isomorphic with the natural number series. [Chapters 4-7] Whether the latter objectively corresponds to characteristics of the physical world remains an open question." [Chapters 1-3]

[The] "excited state . . . contents appear in conjunction with the preconscious aspects of the number archetype." [Chapter 12]

Page 303

"Synchronistic manifestations . . . contain the mystery of the sporadic conjunction of psychic and physical events, revealing a common 'meaning.' This phenomenon seems to hint at the existence of the *unus mundus*, the transcendental unity of existence. In the past men tried to determine the meaning common to these two classes of events by using the rhythms of natural numbers. They worked on the assumption that these numbers illustrated some of the most primitive and basic forms of the spirit. [Chapters 1-3] When we take into account the individual characteristics of natural numbers [Chapters 4-7], we can actually demonstrate that they produce the same ordering effects in the physical and psychic realms; they therefore appear to constitute the most basic constants of nature expressing unitary psychophysical reality." [Chapters 1-3]

Pages 303f.

"Since the concept of the *unus mundus* transcends consciousness, it is represented in mankind's historical *Weltanschauungen* [worldviews] by *symbols*, which most frequently consist of a double mandala portraying both the timeless and time-bound order of existence. [Chapters 10-11] While the timeless order seems to relate to the general concept of acausal orderedness in the physical and psychic realms, the time-bound order refers more to peripheral phenomena, such as synchronistic happenings, that are creative acts in time." [Chapters 1-3]

Page 304

"The two systems are incommensurable, and because of this they form a fitting symbol for the ultimate unity of existence as a *coincidentia oppositorum*." [Chapter 15]

Appendix

Einstein Lite (Relativity 101)

The basic ideas are actually very simple; they just require a different way of looking at things.

Imagine I'm on a train. Let's suppose my train is going 100 miles per hour. Suppose also I am a major league pitcher standing on top of the train, and I can throw the ball at a speed of 100 miles per hour. I throw it in the direction the train is moving. Pretend air resistance does not exist. You are standing alongside the track. When the train with the thrown ball on top of it goes by you, the ball is going 200 miles per hour. The speed of the ball is 200 miles per hour because it is moving at the original speed of the train plus the speed at which I, the great major league pitcher, threw it. If I, the pitcher, had not thrown the ball, if I were simply holding the ball in my hand, when the train went past you the ball would have been moving at 100 miles per hour because that is how fast the train was going. Before the ball was thrown it was moving at the 100 miles per hour of the train. (Figure 18a) Then, when the ball is thrown in the direction of the train's movement, the ball has the speed at which it was going from being on top of the train plus the speed at which it was thrown. The speed of the ball is the train's 100 miles per hour plus the 100 miles per hour speed of the throw. (Figure 18b)

Now let's suppose the train is going along at 150,000 miles per second. I know trains can't go this fast. But suppose they could. (Subatomic particles can go this fast but I'm trying to give an example with elements from our common experience.) Suppose again I am standing on the train and I throw a baseball with a speed of 150,000 miles per second in the direction the train is moving. How fast is that baseball going when it passes you, the observer, on the ground? You might think, by analogy with the above example, that it would be traveling at 300,000 miles per second. The 150,000 miles per second of the movement of the train plus the 150,000 miles per second of the speed of my throw would equal

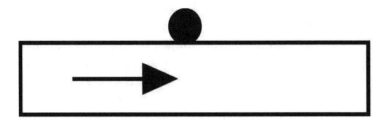

a) The speed of the ball is the speed of the train

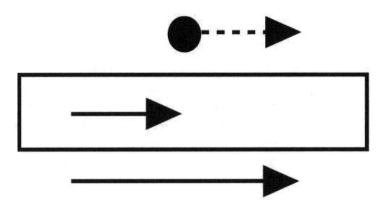

b) The speed of the ball is the speed of the train plus the speed of the pitch (most of the time)

Figures 18a and 18b. The addition of speed for moving bodies.

300,000 miles per second. But the theory of relativity demonstrates that nothing can go faster than the speed of light, which is 186,000 miles per second. What has happened? How can the ball be going 150,000 miles per second for me, the person who threw it, from a train going 150,000 miles a second, and *not* be traveling at those combined speeds when it passes you? How can the speed at which it passes you *not* be 300,000 miles per second? How can the speed of the ball only be 186,000 miles per second for you, the observer?

The reason this can and does happen (in situations where objects can move that fast, for example in subatomic and cosmological research) is that the duration of time and the length of space on the train where I, the pitcher, am is actually different than the duration of time and the length of space on the ground where you, the observer, are standing. Time changes. Space changes. Time on the moving train is longer (time dilation) as it is viewed by the observer on the ground; space on the train is shorter (length contraction) as it is viewed by the observer on the ground.[134]

This lengthening of time has been shown in a way easily demonstrable to our senses, by putting an absolutely accurate clock on a fast-flying jet and then having the jet fly around the world several times. When the jet lands and the time on that clock is compared with another absolutely accurate clock on the ground, the time indicated by the clock that was on the jet will be a little bit different from the time indicated by the stationary clock. The difference is miniscule because the moving jet was not going anywhere near the speed of light, but that small amount is large enough to measure. So the duration of time (and the length of space) is dependent on the speed at which things are moving.[135]

---

[134] "Special Relativity," Virtual Visitor Center.

[135] "In 1971 two physicists, J. C. Hafele and R. E. Keating, used atomic clocks accurate to about one billionth of a second (one nanosecond) to measure the small time dilation that occurs while flying in a jet plane. They flew atomic clocks in a jet for 45 hours, then compared the clock readings to a clock at rest in the laboratory. To within the accuracy of the clocks they used, time dilation occurred for the clocks in the jet as predicted by relativity. Relativistic effects occur at ordinary velocities, but they are too small to measure without extremely precise instruments. ("Special Relativity - Experimental Verification," *Science Encyclopedia)*

Now just look at the room you are in. Imagine I am with you, and I want you to locate a particular point in the room. Say I blindfold you and want to direct you to the top of a chair across the room. I would say walk straight ahead so far, then to the right or left so far, then move your hand up and down by such and such a distance. I had to tell you three distances for your hand to touch the top of the chair: how far straight ahead, how far right (or left), how far up (or down). That is to say, space is defined dimensionally by three values. (Figure 19)

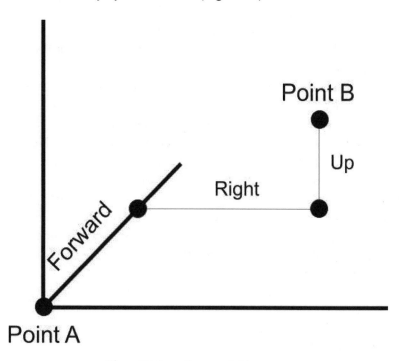

Figure19. Locating a point in space.

But suppose you are moving very, very, very fast through the room. At a particular moment I want to describe to you how far away the top of the chair is when it is precisely in the same position for you as you go by it as it was before. If I gave you three distances as in the previous example, you would never locate it. Why? Because distance is no longer the same for you and me now that you are moving so fast. Lengths in space are not the same anymore. The size of space has changed. So I have to tell you not only three distances but how fast you are going because we have to realize that the size of a length in your fast moving space as I see it is not the same as the size of a length in the space where I am. And vice-versa. We need to know how fast you are moving in order to describe the "length of length" in the space we are each in as we each see it. That is why Einstein calls space "space-time." All these parameters of space, time, and speed (speed is distance per time, e.g., miles per hour) cannot be separated. They exist interdependently.

To describe the location of an object that is moving very fast with respect to you, or that you are moving very fast with respect to, I have to tell you three dimensions in space and I need to tell you the difference in speed between you and the object, because that value will determine what the length of space is within it for your view and within your space for its view. So space-time requires four coordinates to locate a point, where Newton says space requires only three. Newton's three-dimensional physics, as with the stationary room and the stationary chair, works because in his day two things could only move, or be investigated moving, at a very slow speed with respect to each other. Space and time were, or seemed, absolute, but that is no longer so as soon as high speeds (I mean approaching some percentage of the speed of light) are involved.

For Einstein space and time are relative—that is why his 1905 theory is called the "Relativity Theory": the length of an object in an observed place is relative to the difference in speed between the observed and the observer, and the duration of time for an object in an observed place is relative to the speed between the observed and the observer.

The point of all this is to understand how suddenly four becomes the main number in Einstein's physics. It is a highly meaningful "coincidence" that four became the primary number for the Self in Jung's psychology as well, within about ten or fifteen years of Einstein's discovery. Likewise, just twenty-two years before both of them, in 1883, Nietzsche said that the (Trinitarian) God is dead.

The three-world is dying, and our four-world is in the labor of birth.

Figure 20. Marie-Louise von Franz (about 1980).

Acknowledgments

I would like to thank Cynthia Swartz, M.D., and Victoria Cowan for their expert help with the manuscript in process. Sincere appreciation is also due Daryl Sharp's consistently kind support—not to mention the contribution to Jungian psychology made by Inner City Books. Without them many individual voices in our field would never have been heard.

After more than three decades, the master craftsmanship of my teachers in Zürich still astounds me. Preeminent among them was, of course, Marie-Louise von Franz. Her intellectual and analytic expertise, creative sensitivity and vigor, down-to-earth emotional availability, human affability, and downright personal potency will always remain a reference point.

The members of the Indianapolis seminar on *Number and Time* and the analysands who have been willing to share their dreams additionally merit much thanks.

Bibliography

Asimov, Isaac. *Understanding Physics, Volume I: Motion, Sound, and Heat.* New York: New American Library, 1966.

"Benin." Wikipedia. [http://en.wikipedia.org/wiki/Benin]. July 2009.

Calaprice, Alice, ed. *The Expanded Quotable Einstein.* Princeton: Princeton University Press, 2000.

Edinger, Edward F. *The Aion Lectures.* Ed. Deborah Wesley. Toronto: Inner City Books, 1996.

_____. *Anatomy of the Psyche: Alchemical Symbolism in Psychotherapy.* La Salle, IL: Open Court, 1985.

_____. *The Mysterium Lectures.* Ed. Joan Dexter Blackmer. Toronto: Inner City Books, 1995.

_____. *The New God-Image: A Study of Jung's Key Letters Concerning the Evolution of the Western God-Image.* Wilmette, IL: Chiron Publications, 1996.

Eliade, Mircea. *Journal I, 1945-1955.* Trans. Mac Linscott Ricketts. Chicago: University of Chicago Press, 1990.

Eliot, T.S. "Four Quartets." In *The Complete Poems and Plays, 1909-1950.* New York: Harcourt, Brace & World, 1971.

Eranos Homepage – Associazione Amici di Eranos, Ascona. [http://www.eranos.org/content/html/start_english.html]. July 2009.

Evans, Richard I. *Jung on Elementary Psychology: A Discussion between C.G. Jung and Richard I. Evans.* New York: E.P. Dutton, 1976.

"The Fon People." Wikipedia. [http://www.fon.eu/index.htm]. July 2009.

"Geomancy." Wikipedia. [http://en.wikipedia.org/wiki/Geomancy]. July 2009.

Howell, Alice O. *The Heavens Declare: Astrological Ages and the Evolution of Consciousness.* Wheaton, IL: Quest Books, 2006.

Jacobi, Jolande. *The Psychology of C.G. Jung.* New Haven: Yale University Press, 1973.

Jacobsohn, Helmuth, ed. *Timeless Documents of the Soul.* Evanston, IL: Northwestern University Press, 1968.

Jung, C.G. *Children's Dreams: Notes of the Seminar Given in 1936-1940* (Philemon Series). Ed. Lorenz Jung and Maria Meyer-Grass. Trans. Ernst Falzeder and Tony Woolfson. Princeton: Princeton University Press, 2008.

_____. *The Collected Works* (Bollingen Series XX). 20 vols. Trans. R. F. C. Hull. Ed. H. Read, M. Fordham, G. Adler, Wm. McGuire. Princeton: Princeton University Press, 1953-1979.

_____. *Dream Analysis: Notes of the Seminar Given in 1928-1930* (Bolligen Series XCIX). Ed. William McGuire. Princeton: Princeton University Press, 1984.

_____. *Letters* (Bollingen Series XCV). 2 vols. Trans. R.F.C. Hull. Ed. Gerhard Adler, Aniela Jaffé. Princeton: Princeton University Press, 1973.

_____. *Memories, Dreams, Reflections.* Ed. Aniela Jaffé. Trans. Richard and Clara Winston. New York: Vintage Books, 1965.

_____. *Nietzsche's* Zarathustra*: Notes of the Seminar Given in 1934-1939* (Bollingen Series XCIX). 2 vols. Ed. J. L. Jarrett. Princeton: Princeton University Press, 1988.

_____. *Psychologische Interpretation von Kinderträumen und Älterer Literatur über Träume* (a.k.a *Seminar über Kinderträume*) *1938-1939.* Ed. Liliane Frey and Rivkah Schärf. Zürich: privately distributed.

_____. *Visions: Notes of the Seminar Given in 1930-1934* (Bollingen Series XCIX). Vol. 1. Ed. C. Douglas. Princeton: Princeton University Press, 1997.

Kirsch, James. *The Reluctant Prophet.* Los Angeles: Sherbourne Press, 1973.

"Leopold Kronecker." Wikipedia. [http://en.wikipedia.org/wiki/Leopold Kronecker]. July 2009.

Lindorff, David. *Pauli and Jung: The Meeting of Two Great Minds.* Wheaton, IL: Quest Books, 2004.

Lockhart, Russell. "Cancer in Myth and Dream." *Spring 1977.*

Maguire, Anne. *Seven Deadly Sins: The Dark Companions of the Soul.* London: Free Association Books, 2004.

_____. *Skin Disease: A Message from the Soul.* London: Free Association Books, 2004.

March, Robert H. *Physics for Poets.* 2nd ed. Chicago: Contemporary Books, 1978.

"Mary the Jewess." Wikipedia. [http://en.wikipedia.org/wiki/Mary the Jewess]. July 2006.

Máté, Ferenc. *A Vineyard in Tuscany: A Wine Lover's Dream.* Amazon.com. [http://www.amazon.com/Vineyard-Tuscany-Wine-Lovers-Dream/dp/0920256562]. July 2009.

Miller, Barbara S., trans. *The Bhagavad-Gita: Krishna's Counsel in Time of War.* New York: Bantam Books, 1986.

Mitchell, Melanie. *Complexity: A Guided Tour.* Oxford: Oxford University Press, 2009.

Nietzsche, Friedrich. *Thus Spake Zarathustra.* Trans. T. Common. New York: The Modern Library, n.d.

Oxford English Dictionary on CD-ROM. 2nd edition. Oxford: Oxford University Press, 1989.

Pauli, Wolfgang and Jung, C.G. *Atom and Archetype: The Pauli/Jung Letters 1932-1958.* Ed. C.A. Meier. Trans. D. Roscoe. Princeton: Princeton University Press, 2001.

"Postmodernism." Wikipedia. [http://en.wikipedia.org/wiki/Post modernism]. July 2009.

Roach, John. "Internal Clock Leads Monarch Butterflies to Mexico." National Geographic News. June 10, 2003. [http://news.national geographic.com/news/2003/06/0610_030610_monarchs.html]. July 2009.

"The Secret of the Golden Flower." New World Encyclopedia. [http://www.newworldencyclopedia.org/entry/The Secret_of_the Golden Flower]. July 2009.

"Sephirot." Wikipedia. [http://en.wikipedia.org/wiki/Sephirot]. July 2009.

Sharp, Daryl. *Jung Uncorked: Rare Vintages from the Cellar of Analytical Psychology.* Four books. Toronto: Inner City Books, 2008-2009.

Sparks, J. Gary. *At the Heart of Matter: Synchronicity and Jung's Spiritual Testament.* Toronto: Inner City Books, 2007.

"Special Relativity." Virtual Visitor Center. [www2.slac.stanford. edu/vvc/ theory/relativity.html]. July 2009.

"Special Relativity - Experimental Verification," *Science Encyclopedia.* [science.jrank.org/pages/5797/Relativity-Special-Experimental-verification.html]. July 2009.

St. John of the Cross. *Poems of St. John of the Cross.* Trans. Roy Campbell. London: Harvill Press, 1951.

"Taoism." Wikipedia. [http://en.wikipedia.org/wiki/Taoism]. July 2009.

van der Post, Laurens. *Jung and the Story of Our Time.* New York: Vintage Books, 1977.

van Erkelens, Herbert. "Wolfgang Pauli's Dialogue with the Spirit of Matter." *Psychological Perspectives,* no. 24 (Spring Summer 1991).

_____. "Wolfgang Pauli and the Chinese *Anima* Figure." *Eranos Yearbook 1999.* Ed. J.G. Donat, J.F. Livernois. Woodstock, Connecticut: Spring Audio and Journal, 1999.

Virgil. *The Aeneid.* Trans. R. Fitzgerald. New York: Vintage Classics, 1990.

von Franz, Marie-Louise, ed. *Aurora Consurgens.* Trans. R.F.C. Hull and A.S.B. Glover. Toronto: Inner City Books, 2000.

_____. *Creation Myths.* Zürich: Spring Publications, 1975.

_____. *Dreams.* Boston: Shambala, 1991.

_____. *Number and Time: Reflections Leading toward a Unification of Depth Psychology and Physics.* Trans. A. Dykes. Evanston, IL: Northwestern University Press, 1974.

_____. *Psyche and Matter.* Boston: Shambala, 1992.

_____. *Zahl und Zeit: Psychologische Überlegungen zu einer Annäherung von Tiefenpsychologie und Physik.* Stuttgart: Ernst Klett Verlag, 1970.

"Where or When: by Richard Rogers & Lorenz Hart." Lorenz Hart. [http://www.lorenzhart.org/wheresng.htm]. July 2009.

Wilhelm, Richard, trans. *The I Ching or Book of Changes.* Rendered into English by C.F. Baynes. London: Routledge and Kegan Paul, 1968.

Wilhelm, Richard, and C.G. Jung. *The Secret of the Golden Flower.* Trans. R. Wilhelm and C. Baynes. London: Routledge and Kegan Paul, 1962.

Ziegler, Alfred J. *Archetypal Medicine.* Trans. Gary Hartman. Dallas: Spring Publications, 1983.

Index

entries in *italics* refer to illustrations

Also in this Series by Marie-Louise von Franz

AURORA CONSURGENS: On the Problem of Opposites in Alchemy
ISBN 978-0-919123-90-8. (2000) 576pp. **30-page Index** *Sewn* $50
A penetrating commentary on a rare medieval treatise, scattered throughout with insights relevant to the process of individuation in modern men and women.

THE PROBLEM OF THE PUER AETERNUS
ISBN 978-0-919123-88-5. (2000) 288pp. **11 illustrations** *Sewn* $40
The term *puer aeternus* (Latin, eternal youth) is used in Jungian psychology to describe a certain type of man or woman: charming, creative, and ever in pursuit of their dreams. This is the classic study of those who remain adolescent well into their adult years.

THE CAT: A Tale of Feminine Redemption
ISBN 978-0-919123-84-7. (1999) 128pp. **8 illustrations** *Sewn* $25
"The Cat" is a Romanian fairy tale about a princess who at the age of seventeen is bewitched—turned into a cat. . . . One by one von Franz unravels the symbolic threads.

C.G. JUNG: His Myth in Our Time
ISBN 978-0-919123-78-6. (1998) 368pp. **30-page Index** *Sewn* $40
The most authoritative biography of Jung, comprising an historical account of his seminal ideas, including his views on the collective unconscious, archetypes and complexes, typology, creativity, active imagination and individuation.

ARCHETYPAL PATTERNS IN FAIRY TALES
ISBN 978-0-919123-77-9. (1997) 192pp. *Sewn* $30
In-depth studies of six fairy tales—from Spain, Denmark, China, France and Africa, and one from the Grimm collection—with references to parallel themes in many others.

REDEMPTION MOTIFS IN FAIRY TALES
ISBN 978-0-919123-01-4. (1980) 128pp. *Sewn* $25
A nonlinear approach to the significance of fairy tales for an understanding of the process of psychological development. Concise explanations of complexes, projection, archetypes and active imagination. A modern classic.

ON DIVINATION AND SYNCHRONICITY: Psychology of Meaningful Chance
ISBN 978-0-919123-02-1. (1980) 128pp. **15 illustrations** *Sewn* $25
A penetrating study of the psychological aspects of time, number and methods of divining fate such as the I Ching, astrology, Tarot, palmistry, dice, etc. Extends and amplifies Jung's work on synchronicity, contrasting Western attitudes with those of the East.

ALCHEMY: An Introduction to the Symbolism and the Psychology
ISBN 978-0-919123-04-5. (1980) 288pp. **84 illustrations** *Sewn* $40
Designed as an introduction to Jung's weightier writings on alchemy. Invaluable for interpreting images in modern dreams and for an understanding of relationships. Rich in insights from analytic experience.

See last page for discounts and postage/handling

Also in this Series, by Daryl Sharp

Please see last page for discounts and postage/handling.

THE SECRET RAVEN
Conflict and Transformation in the Life of Franz Kafka
ISBN 978-0-919123-00-7. (1980) 128 pp. $25

PERSONALITY TYPES: Jung's Model of Typology
ISBN 978-0-919123-30-9. (1987) 128 pp. **Diagrams** $25

THE SURVIVAL PAPERS: Anatomy of a Midlife Crisis
ISBN 978-0-919123-34-2. (1988) 160 pp. $25

DEAR GLADYS: The Survival Papers, Book 2
ISBN 978-0-919123-36-6. (1989) 144 pp. $25

JUNG LEXICON: A Primer of Terms and Concepts
ISBN 978-0-919123-48-9. (1991) 160 pp. **Diagrams** $25

GETTING TO KNOW YOU: The Inside Out of Relationship
ISBN 978-0-919123-56-4. (1992) 128 pp. $25

THE BRILLIG TRILOGY:

1. CHICKEN LITTLE: The Inside Story *(A Jungian romance)*
ISBN 978-0-919123-62-5. (1993) 128 pp. $25

2. WHO AM I, REALLY? Personality, Soul and Individuation
ISBN 978-0-919123-68-7. (1995) 144 pp. $25

3. LIVING JUNG: The Good and the Better
ISBN 978-0-919123-73-1. (1996) 128 pp. $25

JUNGIAN PSYCHOLOGY UNPLUGGED: My Life as an Elephant
ISBN 978-0-919123-81-6. (1998) 160 pp. $25

DIGESTING JUNG: Food for the Journey
ISBN 978-0-919123-96-0. (2001) 128 pp. $25

JUNG UNCORKED: Rare Vintages from the Cellar of Analytical Psychology
Four vols.. ISBN 978-1-894574-21-1/22-8.. (2008) 128 pp. each. $25 each

THE SLEEPNOT TRILOGY:

1. NOT THE BIG SLEEP: On having fun, seriously *(A Jungian romance)*
ISBN 978-0-894574-13-6. (2005) 128 pp. $25

2. ON STAYING AWAKE: Getting Older and Bolder *(Another Jungian romance)*
ISBN 978-0-894574-16-7. (2006) 144 pp. $25

3. EYES WIDE OPEN: Late Thoughts *(Another Jungian romance)*
ISBN 978-0-894574-18-1.. (2007) 160 pp. $25

Also in this Series, by Edward F. Edinger

Please see last page for discounts and postage/handling.

SCIENCE OF THE SOUL: A Jungian Perspective
ISBN 978-1-894574-03-6. (2002) 128 pp. $25

THE PSYCHE ON STAGE
Individuation Motifs in Shakespeare and Sophocles
ISBN 978-0-919123-94-6. (2001) 96 pp. **Illustrated** $25

EGO AND SELF: The Old Testament Prophets
ISBN 978-0-919123-91-5. (2000) 160 pp. $25

THE PSYCHE IN ANTIQUITY
　Book 1: Early Greek Philosophy
　ISBN 978-0-919123-86-1. (1999) 128 pp. $25
　Book 2: Gnosticism and Early Christianity
　ISBN 978-0-919123-87-8. (1999) 160 pp. $25

THE AION LECTURES: Exploring the Self in Jung's *Aion*
ISBN 978-0-919123-72-4. (1996) 208 pp. **30 illustrations** $30

MELVILLE'S MOBY-DICK: An American Nekyia
ISBN 978-0-919123-70-0. (1995) 160 pp. $25

THE MYSTERIUM LECTURES
A Journey Through Jung's *Mysterium Coniunctionis*
ISBN 978-0-919123-66-3. (1995) 352 pp. **90 illustrations** $40

THE MYSTERY OF THE CONIUNCTIO
Alchemical Image of Individuation
ISBN 978-0-919123-67-6. (1994) 112 pp. **48 illustrations** $25

GOETHE'S FAUST: Notes for a Jungian Commentary
ISBN 978-0-919123-44-1. (1990) 112 pp. $25

THE CHRISTIAN ARCHETYPE A Jungian Commentary on the Life of Christ
ISBN 978-0-919123-27-4. (1987) 144 pp. **34 illustrations** $25

THE BIBLE AND THE PSYCHE
Individuation Symbolism in the Old Testament
ISBN 978-0-919123-23-1. (1986) 176 pp. **20 illustrations** $30

ENCOUNTER WITH THE SELF
A Jungian Commentary on William Blake's *Illustrations of the Book of Job*
ISBN 978-0-919123-21-2. (1986) 80 pp. **22 illustrations** $25

THE CREATION OF CONSCIOUSNESS
Jung's Myth for Modern Man
ISBN 978-0-919123-13-7. (1984) 128 pp. **10 illustrations** $25

Studies in Jungian Psychology
by Jungian Analysts

Quality Paperbacks

Prices and payment in $US (except in Canada, and Visa orders, $Cdn)

Jung Uncorked: Rare Vintages from the Cellar of Analytical Psychology
Four vols. *Daryl Sharp (Toronto)* ISBN 978-1-894574-21-1/22-8. 128 pp. $25 each

Jung and Yoga: The Psyche-Body Connection
Judith Harris (London, Ontario) ISBN 978-0-919123-95-3. 160 pp. $25

The Gambler: Romancing Lady Luck
Billye B. Currie (Jackson, MS) 978-1-894574-19-8. 128 pp. $25

Conscious Femininity: Interviews with Marion Woodman
Introduction by Marion Woodman (Toronto) ISBN 978-0-919123-59-5. 160 pp. $25

The Sacred Psyche: A Psychological Approach to the Psalms
Edward F. Edinger (Los Angeles) ISBN 978-1-894574-09-9. 160 pp. $25

Eros and Pathos: Shades of Love and Suffering
Aldo Carotenuto (Rome) ISBN 978- 0-919123-39-7. 144 pp. $25

Descent to the Goddess: A Way of Initiation for Women
Sylvia Brinton Perera (New York) ISBN 978-0-919123-05-2. 112 pp. $25

Addiction to Perfection: The Still Unravished Bride
Marion Woodman (Toronto) ISBNj 978-0-919123-11-3. Illustrated. 208 pp. $30/$35hc

The Illness That We Are: A Jungian Critique of Christianity
John P. Dourley (Ottawa) ISBN 978-0-919123-16-8. 128 pp. $25

Coming To Age: The Croning Years and Late-Life Transformation
Jane R. Prétat (Providence) ISBN 978-0-919123-63-2. 144 pp. $25

Jungian Dream Interpretation: A Handbook of Theory and Practice
James A. Hall, M.D. (Dallas) ISBN 978-0-919123-12-0. 128 pp. $25

Phallos: Sacred Image of the Masculine
Eugene Monick (Scranton) ISBN 978-0-919123-26-7. 30 illustrations. 144 pp. $25

The Sacred Prostitute: Eternal Aspect of the Feminine
Nancy Qualls-Corbett (Birmingham) ISBN 978-0-919123-31-1. Illustrated. 176 pp. $30

Longing for Paradise: Psychological Perspectives on an Archetype
Mario Jacoby (Zurich) ISBN 978-1-894574-17-4. 240 pp. $35

The Pregnant Virgin: A Process of Psychological Development
Marion Woodman (Toronto) ISBN 978-0-919123-20-5. Illustrated. 208 pp. $30pb/$35hc

<u>*Discounts:*</u> *any 3-5 books, 10%; 6-9 books, 20%; 10-19, 25%; 20 or more, 40% .*

<u>*Add Postage/Handling:*</u> *1-2 books, $6 surface ($10 air); 3-4 books, $8 surface*

($12 air); 5-9 books, $15 surface ($20 air); 10 or more, $15 surface ($30 air)

<u>**Visa credit cards accepted. Toll-free: Tel. 1-888-927-0355; Fax 1-888=924-1814.**</u>

INNER CITY BOOKS

Box 1271, Station Q, Toronto, ON M4T 2P4, Canada

Tel. (416) 927-0355 / Fax (416) 924-1814 / booksales@innercitybooks.net